30119 026 083 98 2

WA.
11/18

BRACELETS

D1513700

BANGLES & BRACELETS

Amanda Doughty

A & C Black • London

Every effort has been made to ensure that all the information in this book is accurate. However, due to differing conditions, tools and individual skills, the publisher and the author cannot be held responsible for any injury, losses or other damages that may result from the use of information in this book. Neither the author nor the publisher can accept any legal liability for any errors or omissions. All safety information and advice contained in this book should be fully adhered to. Jewellery-making can involve the use of dangerous substances and sharp tools. Always follow the manufacturer's instructions, and store chemicals (clearly labelled) and tools well out of the reach of children.

I am extremely grateful to all the artists who have contributed their images to this book, and most particularly to those who have shared their knowledge and expertise by allowing me to use step-by-step instructions for making selected pieces. Obviously, these are included in this book as practice exercises, so that you can learn new techniques, skills and effects by following an experienced teacher, and hopefully use your newly honed skills to work on your own designs and original ideas. Please respect the experience, generosity and copyright of the makers featured by using the designs and instructions included in this book in the spirit of learning; you should never attempt to pass off someone else's original design as your own.

FRONTISPIECE *Double-felt Bangle by Hannah Louise Lamb (Scotland) is made of silver and felt. The silver is roll-printed and fabricated with hand-pierced details and hand-dyed felt. Photo: Hannah L. Lamb.*

TITLE PAGE *This triple bangle by Amanda Doughty (England) is made in silver and 18 ct gold. One gold bangle is made to sit on the inside so that it only shows on occasion.*

CONTENTS PAGE: *Two bracelets by Elizabeth Bone, (England) Photo: Electronic Market Squares, courtesy of the Sonar Project*

First published in Great Britain in 2009
A & C Black Publishers Limited
36 Soho Square
London W1D 3QY
www.acblack.com

ISBN: 978-0-7136-7929-8

Copyright © 2009 Amanda Doughty

Amanda Doughty has asserted her right under the Copyright, Design and Patents Act 1988 to be identified as the author of this work.

Typeset in FB Californian

Book design by James Watson
Cover design by Sutchinda Thompson
Commissioning Editor: Susan James
Managing Editor: Sophie Page

CIP Catalogue records for this boo
from the British Library and the L
Congress.

All rights reserved. No part of th
may be reproduced in any form o
graphic, electronic, or mechanica
photocopying, recording, taping
storage and retrieval systems – w
permission in writing of the pub.

LONDON BOROUGH OF SUTTON LIBRARY SERVICE (SUT)	
30119 026 083 98 2	
Askews	Oct-2010
739.278	

hat is made
inable forests.
le. The
s conform
he country

Contents

ACKNOWLEDGEMENTS

Firstly my thanks must go especially to the project contributors: Lise Bech, Rachel Dorris, Melissa Hunt, Sarah Keay, Lindsey Mann, Jean Scott-Moncrieff and John Moore – they made it feel so much less about work and more about a sharing of skills between friends and fellow makers. Their valuable time, efforts, energy and expertise have been incredible. Each maker has unselfishly shared their knowledge of their technique and experience, which has been developed over years in their practice. By demonstrating their valued projects they enable us to learn directly from their experiences. Their generosity has taught me a new respect for a subject in which I realise I still have so much to learn and explore. It was especially interesting for me, where possible, to visit workshops and see a different way of making, talking to the jeweller in detail and appreciating a different approach.

I also owe thanks to the many jewellers worldwide who kindly sent in bangle or bracelet images as well as offers to demonstrate their projects; I was really sorry not to be able to fit them all in the book. My special thanks must go to the American jewellers who went to huge efforts to send in images, captions and detailed explanations. There was such an amazing selection overall that I was both humbled and excited to realise just how many talented makers there are making beautiful and interesting work. The projects, as well as the images, were chosen according to the breadth and suitability that I could offer the reader in this particular book, but they are also projects that I found interesting and inspiring. So many exciting images were submitted that unfortunately I could not justifiably squeeze them all in.

My thanks also go to Susan James for the opportunity of writing this book, for her guidance and allowing me to treat the book as my own without feeling of the constraints of a publisher behind me.

Thanks also to Angie Boothroyd, fellow jeweller and author of *Necklaces and Pendants* in the same Jewellery Handbook series, for her friendship and encouragement – Angie's book became something to aspire to whilst completing this book; to Stuart Paul, a talented goldsmith and craftsman whom I have learnt a great deal from, who has generously shared a vast amount of his knowledge, some of which is detailed in this book; to Stewart Drew, my husband, for being an enormous support, and also my photographer (all photos are his work unless otherwise stated) and picture editor; and finally to my family and friends, for tirelessly listening to me and supporting me through the writing of this book, without whose encouragement it would not have been possible.

Introduction

This is by no means the definitive book on bangle- and bracelet-making; I would not have embarked on such a project or suggested that it was possible for me to do so. Instead it is an exploration.

I have always enjoyed making bangles. A bangle is a perfect 'large, wearable ornament', which when worn you can fully appreciate yourself; unlike a pair of earrings, for example, which are mostly to be appreciated by the onlooker. Of course, this does not take into account the enjoyment you get from jewellery when you are not wearing it – jewellery as a beautiful object in its own right – but that is another book altogether.

A bangle is a rigid, ring-shaped bracelet usually made without a clasp so as to slip over the hand, but sometimes having a hinged opening and a clasp.

A bracelet is an ornamental band or circlet, worn for decoration for the wrist or arm or, sometimes, for the ankle. Of course, every designer has the right to call their jewellery whatever they prefer, whatever they believe fits the piece. Strictly speaking, a bangle might indeed be a bracelet and vice versa.

For this book I have chosen to include the expertise of other jewellers so as to demonstrate their knowledge and craft. Please do not copy these projects directly; they have been generously shared in good faith. Instead please learn from them and take away this new knowledge, pushing it in a unique and interesting direction.

In addition, the book is also scattered with a range of innovative examples of work in a variety of materials to provide additional context and inspiration.

Not every tool used in each of the projects has been itemised; it is presumed that you have basic tools and equipment. The Basic Jewellery Techniques chapter, page 9, shows images of tools and provides information on their use. Any unusual or specialist tools specific to the chapter project have been photographed or itemised at the head of each chapter.

Finally, health and safety guidelines have been included in each chapter to avoid accidents and to remind jewellers that there are no exceptions: health and safety must always remain paramount.

This bracelet *by Yoko Shimizu (Italy) is constructed in silver, 24 ct gold and niello.*
Photo: Federico Cavicchioli.

Basic Jewellery Techniques
by Amanda Doughty

This book will not show every aspect and technique of jewellery-making. Instead its primary concern is to give the reader a sound level of understanding about the projects set out in each chapter, and in that regard the reader is assumed to have basic jewellery-making knowledge and skills. This chapter is here for quick reference, and to brush up skills if necessary, and is particularly geared towards understanding the making of bangles and bracelets, especially a bangle that will form part of the project demonstrated in Chapter 8.

Images of a jewellery toolbox and workshop equipment in their entirety are not pictured in this basic jewellery chapter, as just the tools that are specific to the projects in this book would make a very extensive list. I have included a few specialist tools that I frequently use, which might not necessarily be found in a general workshop – for example, a flatting press, a disc sander and a bangle stretcher. These three tools are invaluable for bangle-making, as they speed up the process; however, basic hand tools and equipment are equally as good, just a little slower.

Where necessary and appropriate, both in the detailing of the pictures and in the making notes, there are detailed alternatives or reasons for using and choosing specific equipment. Jewellery-making being a profession where time is quite often of the essence, be it for a commission or simply to make the piece affordable by saving time, it is hoped that tips or shortcuts might be gathered from this chapter.

Sometimes machines can be purchased that are not specifically for jewellery-making, but are more affordable and can be adapted for purpose. For example, the belt sander, which I frequently use to sand down my work, is from Tilgear, an engineering and woodworking company (see page 15 for details and see the suppliers' list at the end of the book for details). However, it is important to be certain that the machine you are interested in is suitable for requirements and appropriate for your needs before committing yourself to buying it.

These basic jewellery techniques are based on my knowledge and experience; they are not necessarily the conclusive method. You only need to glance at a few other jewellery books to gather that there are many possibilities. For example, there are a number of ways to solder, just as there are a number of ways to boil an egg.

Over the years I have experienced a wealth of different approaches and methods; the most valuable knowledge has been gathered from fellow makers, and also from students I have taught, whom other jewellers have previously taught. I have also taken further classes, as a student, to widen my knowledge base. Enriched by these accumulated skills, I have adapted my approach to the best of my ability so far, knowing that there is still a great deal to accomplish.

Ultimately, jewellery-making is all about patience, practice, trial and error, whilst never compromising on design, quality and finish.

TOOLS OF THE TRADE

1. Binding wire.
2. Charcoal blocks.
3. Reversible tweezers held in a vice called a third hand.
4. Sievert torch with larger head – the smaller head is not always large enough for soldering bangles.

> **TIP** Small handheld torches are incredibly useful for soldering small items, although not for bangle-making.

5. Borax cone, brush and solder.

> **TIP** Solder paste is very useful – solder and flux in paste form – it comes in a syringe and is brilliant for jump rings and very fine soldering. However, be aware that it can burn out and leave tiny holes if you overheat it. Auflux can be used as a flux as an alternative to borax.

6. Heat bricks: asbestos substitute and honeycomb board.
7. Tin snips.
8. Solder probe.
9. Fine tweezers.
10. Metal turntable.

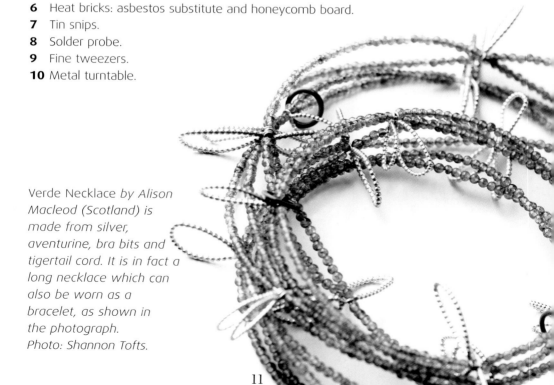

Verde Necklace by Alison Macleod (Scotland) is made from silver, aventurine, bra bits and tigertail cord. It is in fact a long necklace which can also be worn as a bracelet, as shown in the photograph. Photo: Shannon Tofts.

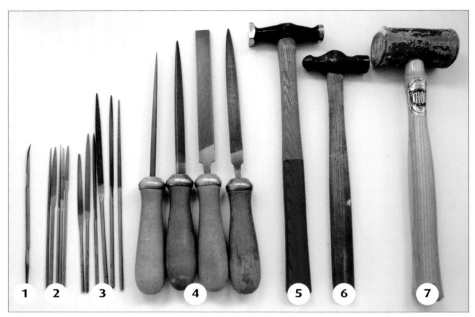

(1)Riffler file; (2)five escapement files; (3)six needle files; two sizes; (4)four hand files with handles; (5)planishing hammer; (6)basic metal hammer with a textured head; (7)rawhide mallet.

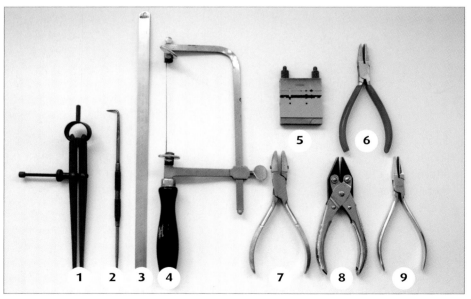

(1)Dividers; (2)scriber; (3)metal ruler; (4)adjustable saw frame and blade; (5)Chenier clamp; (6)half-round pliers; (7)nylon pliers; (8)parallel pliers; (9)flat-nosed pliers.

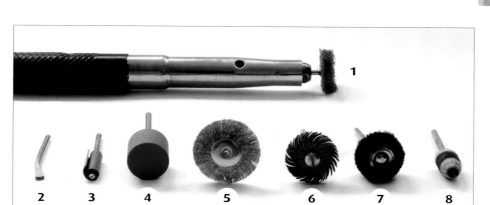

1 Hand piece of pendant drill fitted with a screw-thread mandrel and a matting scourer attached.

TIP This is a more cost-effective way of making your own matting scourer from a green kitchen scourer and a screw-thread mandrel. Simply cut a piece of kitchen scourer into a circle, push onto the screw-thread mandrel and secure in place.

---

2 Small handmade hammerhead attachment, very good for filling tiny holes in castings and seams.

3 Split mandrel with emery paper.

4 Eveflex long-lasting high-performance polishers, available in four grades: extra fine (shown here), fine, medium and coarse.

TIP It is much better to make your own split mandrel, as the slot is smaller and tighter and the paper stays in better. Simply cut the top off a worn-out pendant attachment; usually brass wheel or calico attachments are better for this (the metal appears to be softer). Carefully pierce a line down the middle of the rod three quarters of the way down. Then slot your emery paper in as usual.

---

5 Brass wheel.

6 Radial abrasive disc, ideal for cleaning, pre-polishing and texturing (available in different grades).

7 Wool polishing mop.

8 Hard felt polishing mop.

(1)Flat plate; (2)bangle gauge; (3)bangle sizer (similar in principal to a ring sizer); (4)cast-iron round triblet; (5)bangle stretcher; (6)flatting press.

1 Belt sander with special belt for metal from 3M products. The round disc is very coarse abrasive paper.

2 Pickling equipment: heated ring, wire gauze, lidded Pyrex dish, alum or safety pickle, and plastic tweezers. Alum is an alternative to safety pickle and can be purchased from chemists; it is very good for silver and gold.

Important: It is very important to have wire gauze between the heated ring and dish, as this prevents overheating, and possible breakage of, the dish. Many jewellers use a slow cooker.

3 Single-barrel polisher, suitable for limited needs, though a double one or a heavier-duty barrel polisher might be advisable for greater use. There are also other polishers on the market, including a magnetic or disc-finishing polisher. Check with suppliers.

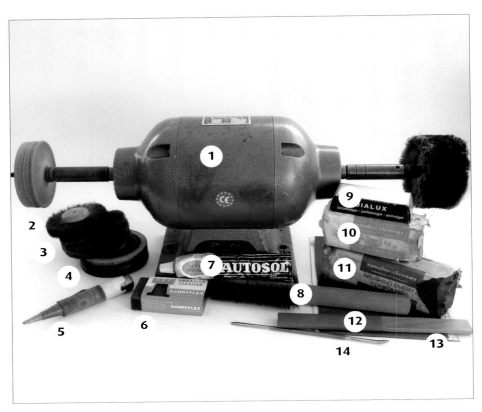

1 Polishing motor with used Artifex rubber wheel on left and used calico mop on right.
2 Fine brass wire circular brushes.
3 Scotch-Brite satinising mop.
4 Used hard polishing mop.
5 Polishing motor shaft with emery paper attached. Ideal for use on the inside of bangles and the outside for very flat edges where the surface needs removing. The emery paper is carefully taped to the shaft with masking tape, and torn off when exhausted. Great care must be taken when using this technique.
6 Garryflex, an abrasive rubber block used for matting metal, available in different grades: fine, medium, coarse and extra coarse.
7 Autosol, an extremely useful cream cleaner if you have limited polishing equipment, can be purchased from car suppliers.
8 Brass brush, good for a wired finish.
9 Green Dialux, a high grade polishing compound used for platinum, steel or other hard white metals.
10 Hyfin, traditionally used for polishing stainless steel, is also very good for

precious metals and is the cleaner to use in the workshop, in preference to tripoli or rouge.

11 Brushing emery compound, traditionally used for initial polishing of most metals.

12 Emery paper and stick.

13 Glass sheet, used as a flat plate, and emery paper.

14 Burnisher.

TIP Special 3M product 'finishing film' and flexible backed emery paper are very useful instead of emery paper. Check with suppliers.

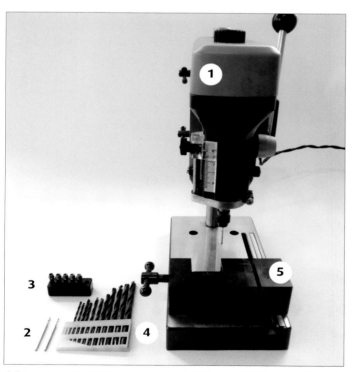

(1)Bench drill; (2)two mounted drills on 2.35 mm (less than 0.093 in.) shanks; (3)five collets; (4)drill bits of various sizes; (5)steel vice. This particular bench drill is fairly basic and only makes holes up to 3 mm (0.118 in.); if you are using a drill frequently and need accuracy it is worth investing in a more precise one which allows for larger drill bits.

> **TIP** If you are simply making small holes use a pendant motor, a basic hand drill or a bow drill.

HEALTH AND SAFETY

Great care must be taken when working in the workshop, especially with any unfamiliar tools and machinery: long hair must be tied back, goggles must be worn when using machinery and loose clothing must be removed.

MAKING A SIMPLE SILVER BANGLE

This project demonstrates step by step how a simple silver bangle is made, describing how to size a bangle, and how to pierce, file, solder, anneal, clean up and finish the metal.

It has been devised especially to freshen up your making skills, if necessary, and is not complicated, making a bangle is rather like making a huge ring. The project will describe the process and where necessary discuss in greater detail some relevant points and tips.

CHOOSING THE METAL

For making bangles I often buy metal in a long length, in wire form, by the meter, and divide it up. However, the range of metal gauge available in wire form from most bullion suppliers is limited, so depending on the design of the bangle you may find it necessary to purchase a long wide sheet and divide it into strips. If you are using sheet metal, a pair of dividers, or a scriber and metal ruler, is used to mark out accurately before piercing.

It is usually cheaper to buy sheet metal rather than wire due to the additional machining/manufacturing costs involved in making wire. When buying sheet metal it makes sense to ask the suppliers to guillotine it into suitable strips; there is usually a small fee added for cutting, but it is worth the additional cost as it saves time and saw blades. However, be aware that there will be a soft guillotined edge on one side of the cut sheet metal, but this can usually be either filed off or carefully hidden inside the bangle.

A huge range of metal widths and depths can be used for making bangles. The suggested metal gauge should be above 0.5 mm (0.02 in.) to avoid the bangle being too flimsy, and thus becoming bent and distorted on the wrist when worn. If the piece is to be worn, the weight, comfort and suitability must be a consideration in the design process. Of course, this does not necessarily apply to all bangles and bracelets, but depends entirely on their purpose.

1 Sizing the bangle

This project uses flat wire 0.84mm thick x 6 mm wide(0.033 x 0.236 in.). The average bracelet size is approximately 19 or 20 cm (7.48 or 7.87 in.). There are two types of bangle sizers available: one is very basic, rather like a belt that is clipped up and then tried on; the other is rather like a giant ring sizer, and uses a method similar to sizing a ring, although helpfully the bangle sizer has the centimetres required for the bangle length written on each piece.

The finished bangle needs to sit comfortably on the wrist: it must not be so loose that it hangs around and over the thumb, but equally it must not be so tight so that it is too difficult to get on. The bangle sizer must fit comfortably over the thumb knuckle. When establishing the length of the metal required, remember that if the metal gauge is very thick, length must be added to the wire/sheet to compensate. If you are unsure, use the equation for measuring a ring: diameter + depth of metal gauge x π (3.142).

2 Cutting the wire

Wherever possible metal should always be pierced, as it looks neater and will avoid extra work later on. A guillotine or tin snips will distort the metal, and the cut edges will need straightening out really carefully, usually with parallel pliers or gentle hammering.

Loading a saw blade and piercing

Fine blades are used on delicate sheet work, and coarser ones on thicker metal or other materials, for example, plastics. The correct-sized blade is approximately two and a half teeth per thickness of the metal to be pierced.

a) The correct saw blade for the job is chosen. These vary in thickness, from the finest, 6/0, through 5/0, 4/0, 3/0. 2/0, 1/0, 0, 1, 2, 3, 4, 5 to 6, the coarsest.
b) The teeth must run down towards the handle and face outwards.
c) One end of the blade is clamped in place and the screw is tightened.
d) The handle is held and the framework is pushed up against the bench, so that the blade can be fitted into the gap, between the screw and the frame and then

tightened into place. The blade should be taut, and when plucked it should make a 'ping' sound like a violin string.

e) The metal to be pierced should be horizontal on the bench peg and securely held.

TIP An adjustable saw frame is recommended; adjusting the frame can sometimes allow for reuse of shorter, partly broken blades. Deep-throated saw frames are very useful for piercing quite long pieces of metal.

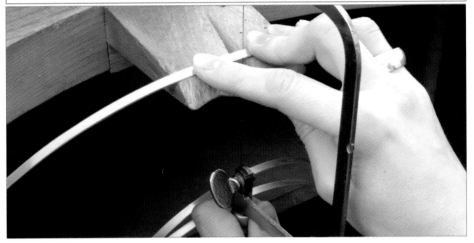

Piercing the wire.

f) The blade is initially run upwards once or twice against the metal edge where piercing is to begin, which creates a starting point.

g) The blade should travel at a right angle to the piece.

h) The grip is relaxed a little and the blade is left to do the work; clenching or jerking the frame could snap the blade. The cut is on the downward motion.

i) When gripping the metal, fingers must be kept away from the cutting line; they must never rest in front of the blade.

TIP If necessary, beeswax can be used as a lubricant; the blade is run through the wax once or twice, care is taken not to clog the teeth. Alternatively, use 'burr life', which is a recommended lubricant (available from Cooksons, see suppliers).

---

3 Either end of the wire is filed

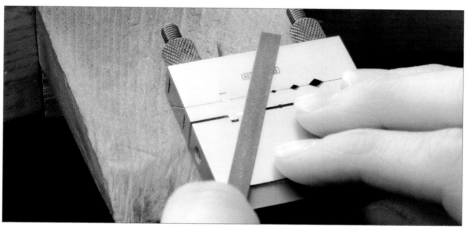

Filing the end of the wire.

This can be done by eye, though it is much more accurate to use a device called a Chenier clamp, ensuring both ends are perfectly met.

Filing is done using a file, either a 6- or 8-inch hand file with a wooden handle, a needle file or a very fine escapement file. The appropriate-sized file must always be used for the job, in this instance a needle file.

Files are available in different shapes and coarseness of cut: pillar (flat), barrette (safety back), half-round, crossing, three-square, knife, square, round and warding. They are graded by number, from 00 (coarsest) to 6 (very fine). Riffler files are also available; these have shaped and curved file blades, and are designed to file awkward and intricate shapes.

a) The work to be filed must be stable, resting on the bench peg.
b) The teeth on files point away from the handle, and the cut is on the forward stroke.
    The file runs along the contour of the metal.
c) On the return stroke the file is lifted, or pressure is eased.
d) The process is repeated until the work is complete.

4 The ends are soldered together
Soldering is the term used for the joining of two pieces of metal together using a special metal alloy, called solder. When solder is heated to a certain temperature it melts and creates a join.

Silver solder is available in five grades: enamelling, hard, medium, easy and extra easy. Their melting points range from 800° to 667° Celsius. There is a wide range of solders available for different metals, carat qualities and colours. Hard solder is used for this project.

a) The metal is clean, free from grease and there are no gaps between the surfaces to be joined. Solder will not flow if both pieces are not touching.

b) Metal can move slightly when heated, and binding wire or reverse tweezers are used to keep the surfaces together if necessary. Alternatively, the metal is annealed and pickled first to relieve tension and avoid too much movement.

c) Borax is mixed and applied to the area to be soldered.

d) The metal is positioned on the block.

e) The solder is cut into pallions approximately 1 mm (0.039 in.) square and applied with the brush positioned across or in the join.

f) The gas torch is turned on and the metal is gently warmed.

g) The borax may bubble and misplace the solder pallions; if necessary they are repositioned with tweezers.

h) The entire piece of metal is gently heated up; it is the heat of the actual metal that melts the solder, enabling it to flow along the join. It is not by directly heating the solder pallions that allows the solder to flow. To ensure a good connection, the flame is moved closer towards the join when the solder starts to melt.

i) Once it has been successfully soldered, it is left to cool.

j) It is then placed in a pickling solution (see stage 5 on page 23).

The solder melting, joining the metal together.

Annealing

This is the process of heating metal to relieve the stresses within it, altering the crystal structure and rendering the metal softer and easier to work with, until it becomes 'hard' again. Work-hardening is the process by which metal becomes harder and more brittle as it is repeatedly hammered, rolled, drawn, twisted or bent. Annealing it again will enable it to become more workable.

To anneal metal, the work is gradually heated up by the torch flame; sterling silver and gold to a dull red, and red gold, copper and brass to a medium red. The flame is removed, and when the faint red has clearly disappeared the metal is quenched in water. Cooling the metal in the air is said to increase hardness (although I have not always found this to be the case). Steel needs to be a very bright red, and should then be left to cool.

5 The metal is pickled

The alum is gently heated, although not to a boil. The metal is left in the pickle for approximately 10 minutes, or until all oxide is removed. The metal is then rinsed in water and dried thoroughly.

Alum, a powder that can be purchased from chemists, is an ideal pickle for silver and gold. Safety pickle is also very useful and the one most commonly used; it can be purchased from suppliers. However, it can sometimes become contaminated more easily than other pickles for reasons I have never quite understood, but which may be due to the residue of steel in tubing that I often use. Important: never put steel tweezers into the pickle solution, always use plastic or brass.

6 The join is filed inside and outside

Filing as per stage 3 (page 21), a needle file is used: a flat file on the outside of the join and a half-round file on the inside. After filing, emery paper is used to smooth the filed surface. A flat emery stick is used on the outside surface and a half-round emery stick is used for the inside. Emery sticks are made by carefully covering a hard wooden stick in double-sided tape and attaching emery paper, ensuring there are no overlaps or creases. Alternatively, emery sticks can be purchased from suppliers.

7 The bangle is shaped on the mandrel

The bangle on the mandrel.

The bangle is placed onto the metal bangle mandrel, and using a rawhide mallet the bangle is gently and evenly hammered. A metal hammer should not be used unless a textured finish is required. The bangle must be turned over on the mandrel; otherwise the bangle becomes slightly tapered like the mandrel. A wooden mandrel can be used, although this will mark and dent much quicker than a cast-iron one. However, it is very useful for hollow forms (for use see chapter 6, Jean Scott-Moncrieff). Oval mandrels are also available.

8 The bangle is stretched

The bangle is then gently stretched on the bangle stretcher, again being turned over during stretching to ensure the bangle does not become tapered. If a bangle stretcher is not available, the bangle can be stretched manually on the mandrel above in stage 7.

9 The entire inside of the bangle is cleaned up

A half-round emery stick is used on the inside surface, first with coarse paper then working down through the grades to finer paper. The emery-papered spindle on the polishing motor or the pendant drill will hugely speed up this process.

The bangle on the bangle stretcher.

24

10 *The bangle is flattened*

The bangle in the flatting press.

The bangle is laid onto the flatting press base and the red handle is firmly pressed downwards; the two flat surfaces will trap and harden the bangle. However, this action must not be repeated too many times, as the bangle will begin to buckle inwards or outwards. Five or six times is sufficient, with the bangle being checked after each pressing for signs of buckling. Should this occur, the buckling should be hammered out with a rawhide mallet on the steel mandrel. Alternatively, the bangle can be flattened on a steel flat plate using a rawhide mallet.

11 *The outside surface is cleaned and the fire stain is removed*

The Artifex wheel is used on the polishing motor, removing the top layer of metal on the outside of the bangle, paying special attention to removing the fire stain. Starting with the coarser Artifex wheel, then moving on to the finer one. Alternatively, a hand file then the emery-papered spindle or the pendant drill can be used in place of the Artifex wheels.

The bangle on the polishing motor with artifex wheel.

12 The edges are cleaned

The edges are made flat using the belt sander, then fine emery paper on a flat stick. This can also be done either on a large glass flat plate covered in emery paper or with a flat stick, working from a medium-coarse paper down to a fine one. The fine Artifex wheel with the bangle angled on the edge is also very useful. By this method all fire stain, file marks and imperfections are removed from the entire bangle.

13 The bangle is polished

The bangle is polished with Hyfin on the polishing motor, and then soaked in warm soapy water. Hyfin is applied to a calico mop, or if preferred tripoli then rouge can be used. If a very high polish is required, brushing emery compound on a separate mop is used prior to the Hyfin. The piece should be held securely in leather to avoid the heat of the metal.

> **TIP** All polishes and mops must be kept separately; this prevents coarser polishes contaminating finer ones. Between polishing processes the piece should be soaked in warm soapy water to remove any polishing compound, then washed and dried thoroughly.

Silver and 18 ct gold bangle by Amanda Doughty photo: Jeremy Johns.

A matt finish

It is important to note that a matt finish will not remain matt when the bangle is worn, just as a highly polished finish will not remain highly polished; eventually, after wear, the two finishes will look similar. This is particularly the case with rings and bangles, which get more wear and tear; earrings and pendants do not tend to suffer to the same extent.

To achieve a matt finish, you should polish the metal thoroughly first, as a matt finish will not hide any imperfections. A variety of techniques can be used to achieve this: wire wool, pumice powder, Garryflex, frosting wheels or Scotch-Brite, by hand, on the polishing motor or pendant motor.

TIP To avoid after-sales disappointment, always make sure the client is fully aware that a matt finish is not permanent. If a hand-finish is applied, the client can be advised how to maintain the finish themselves.

14 The bangle is hardened

The bangle is then placed in the barrel polisher for approximately two hours to harden fully; this also cleans up the inside of the bangle.

TIP Polishing can be outsourced. There are some very good polishers in the trade, who for a reasonable price will achieve a perfect finish that might otherwise take you much longer. See the list of suppliers at the end of the book for details.

Satin Bangles *by Jane Adam (England). These bangles are made of anodised, dyed and milled aluminium. Photo: Joël Degen.*

1. Willow Bangle by Lise Bech

INTRODUCTION

A fascinating project, using very few tools, this bangle is beautifully crafted from willow and will appeal to those of an environmental bent. It is the ideal project for demonstrating how our hands are indeed our best tool.

The resulting bangle has a bold sensitivity, with a unique quality that could not be achieved in any other material.

TOOLS AND MATERIALS

Specialist Materials
Side-cutters and bodkin. Alternatively, you can use a knitting needle, a screwdriver or even a pencil in place of the bodkin, and secateurs or scissors in place of the side-cutters.

Materials
Four to eight rods of very thin willow 60–80 cm (23.62–31.50 in.) long, or more if you are not using the full length. The willow can be fresh, cut within the previous six to eight weeks, or bought dry and soaked in cold water for three to four days. Weeping willow produces suitable rods, as do many other willows, which any local basket-maker can supply (see the list of suppliers for details).

HEALTH & SAFETY

Care must be taken to avoid working in a very confined space, and you should never work near small children.

Terminology: the thick end is called the 'butt' and the thin end the 'tip'.

METHOD

1

Four to eight matching rods are selected. The fibres are softened by stroking and slightly bending the thick end over the thumb, following the natural curve of the rod.

Alternatively, the rod can be wrapped around a wine bottle, rolling pin or similar form. If the rod kinks it is discarded and another rod is chosen.

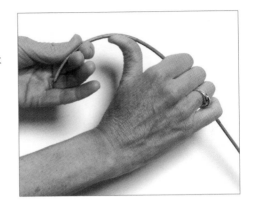

2a

The first rod is held with the butt end in the left hand. With the right hand a downward loop is created and the rod is crossed over and in front of the butt.

2b

While the left hand holds the crossing rods firmly, the right hand guides the tip into the loop from behind, in effect tying a knot.

2c

The knot is tightened/the loop is closed as close to the butt end as possible. This loop should fit easily over the hand, e.g. around 9 cm (3.54 in.) in diameter.

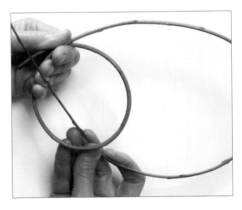

3a

This new 'crossing place' is held with the left fingertips and the tip is guided in a generous curve through the hoop from the back, then tightened.

3b

This is repeated once or twice more, whereupon the tip should now be back near the butt. In other words, each circumnavigation of the hoop requires three or four twists or wraps to complete.

4a

The tip continues to be wound round the hoop, allowing it to travel in the groove created by the previous wraps.

4b

With 10 cm (3.94 in.) left, the tip is fastened away between the previous rounds, through a gap opened up with the bodkin.

5

The hoop is turned anticlockwise and the second rod is inserted from the front, approximately one third of the way along from the original butt end. Stage 3 is then repeated.

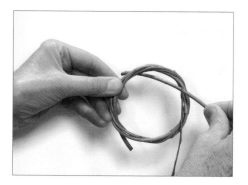

This first turn secures the rod and then stages 3 to 4 are repeated.

6

The hoop is turned anticlockwise by a further third of its circumference, and the butt of the third weaver is inserted in the groove. Stages 3 to 4 are repeated.

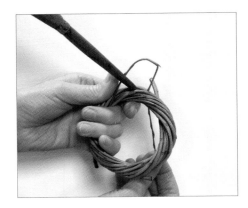

7

When the rods are 80 cm (31.50 in.), on average three rounds can be achieved from each rod; if the bracelet is to be thin, four rods are sufficient. In this instance, the bracelet is turned over, face down on the table.

The butt ends are trimmed by levering them up and cutting each end at a slope so that it lies sweet and flush with the looping.

The tips are then trimmed.

To achieve a fuller shape new rods are inserted and weaving continues as above, trimming after every three or four rods.

Advice: The bracelet is worn with the cut ends facing down towards the fingers/hand.

Step-by-step photography by Narada Ian Ramsey.

Willow bangle, *Lise Bech, Photo: Shannon Tofts.*

Lise Bech at work in her workshop. Photo: Shannon Tofts.

Lise Bech lives and works in the Southern Uplands of Scotland, where she grows a wide range of willows, for her basket-making. Her work celebrates a life lived simply and close to nature and a deep belief in the importance of sustainability and ethical production. Lise exhibits throughout the UK with occasional forays into European and US galleries. A list of current and future shows can be found at www.bechbaskets.net.

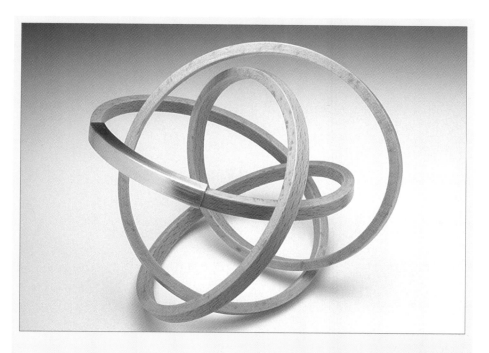

Here Mette T. Jensen's, (England), Top of tree *bangle demonstrates how wood can be bent and formed. The silver is used as a connection and to contrast with the wood. The surface is finished with several layers of oil and wax. Photo: Joël Degen.*

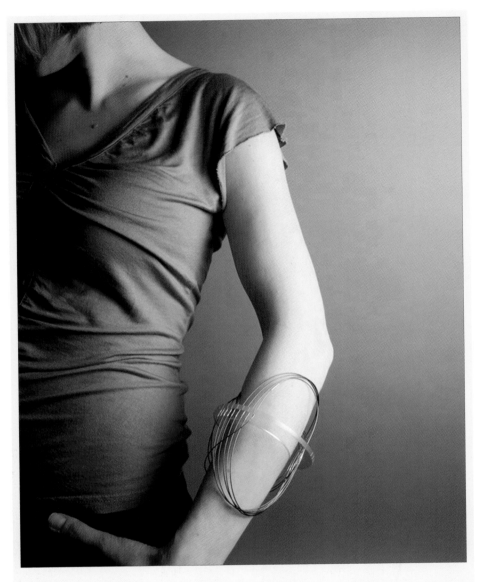

Lunar Bracelet 1, *by Kathryn Marchbank (England) is made from 5 mm transparent Perspex, stainless steel nylon coated wire, silver tube and hand dyed. Initially hand drawn and cut in Perspex, for final production the shapes were traced into Adobe Illustrator® and laser cut forming the solid structure of the bracelet/cuff. The Perspex was drilled and the wire threaded through, fastened and dip dyed by hand. Photo: Juliet Sheath.*

2. Multi-bell bracelet by Rachel Dorris

INTRODUCTION

This bracelet has been made using 16 handmade silver pods and labradorite gemstone beads threaded onto 'tiger tail' wire.

The pods are cleverly achieved by distorting a domed shape, a technique that Rachel has discovered and perfected through much experimentation. The subtle purple labradorites give the bracelet a preciousness only achieved by gemstones, perfectly complementing the handmade silver pods.

This bracelet has a graceful and delicate quality, and moves beautifully when worn on the wrist.

TOOLS AND MATERIALS

Specialist tools

Doming block and punches.

Specialised cutters for the tiger tail and specialised pliers for the crimps.

Other tools and equipment
- Centre punch
- Scotch-Brite™ pad
- Soldering equipment
- Basic jewellery tools and equipment

Materials
- Sufficient silver sheet 0.5 mm (0.02 in.) thick to make 16 circles with diameters of approximately 2 x 8 mm (0.315 in.), 5 x 10 mm (0.394 in.), 6 x 12 mm (0.472 in.) and 3 x 15 mm (0.591 in.).
- A strand of 3 mm (0.118 in.) labradorite gemstone beads.
- Tiger tail and crimps (the bracelet length is 18 cm (7.09 in.)).

HEALTH & SAFETY

Special care must be taken when piercing and soldering. Health & Safety techniques must be adhered to, please see Basic Jewellery Techniques chapter.

METHOD

1
The circles are marked out for the pods on a 0.5 mm (0.02 in.) thick silver sheet.

A centre punch is used to mark the middle of the circle and dividers are used to scribe the circles to be pierced. There are four different disc sizes to be made – 16 in total: 2 x 8 mm (0.315 in.), 5 x 10 mm (0.394 in.), 6 x 12 mm (0.472 in.) and 3 x 15 mm (0.591 in.) in diameter.

TIP: Care is taken when marking out the circles on the silver sheet, so as not to waste too much metal. However, it is important to leave at least enough room for the blade to pass generously through the gaps.

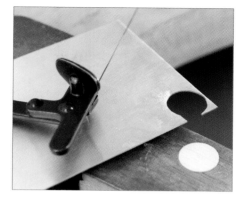

2

The circles are pierced out from the silver sheet with a piercing saw frame and blade.

3

Using a flat needle file, the edges of circles are filed to improve the round shape. Care is taken not to file away too much, thus leaving the circle too small.

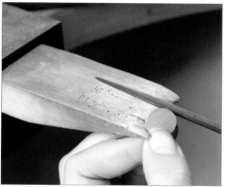

All 16 silver circles are now pierced out and filed. From now on these will be called discs and later referred to as 'pods'.

4

A doming block with deep holes is used to make the domes. The silver disc is placed inside one of the larger holes and an appropriately sized punch is hammered down onto the disc to curve it. The curved disc is then moved into a smaller dome and again an appropriately sized punch is used to dome it.

Through the process of moving the silver disc down the line of holes in the block, and doming it in each one, the disc is formed into as deep a dome as possible.

It is important that the discs are steeply curved. During this process, the silver disc should be annealed once or twice to ensure that it remains workable.

> **TIP** Care is taken to ensure that the centre-punch mark is on the outer surface of the domed disc. Therefore the mark is facing down in the doming block, making it much easier to clean up at a later point.

> **TIP** Good-quality doming punches are used to ensure the interior of domed silver pieces are smooth. If rough ones are used, the silver domes will require a lot of polishing on the inside, which is not easy to do.

5

The domed disc is rested against the bench peg with the edges upwards; the rim is then filed flat using a wide flat file. This is repeated with the other 15 discs.

6

File marks are smoothed from the edges, using emery paper. The outsides of the domes are then also smoothed with emery paper until any existing marks are removed.

7

A pair of parallel pliers are used to squash the domed discs into pod shapes. The ends of the pliers are wrapped with masking tape to protect the silver. Great care is taken not to distort the pod shape or to squash it too much.

8

The jump-ring ends are closed together and a flat surface is filed on the edge where the two ends meet, directly on top of the join.

9

The pods are prepared for soldering by filing a tiny flat surface on top of the punch mark on the outside, therefore filing away the punch mark and leaving a flat surface ideal for soldering.

10

Using hard solder, the jump rings are soldered to the pod.

TIP Care should be taken when soldering. The jump ring is delicate and has a tendency to melt when overheated. To avoid this, the pod is gently heated with the solder pallion on it. With a steady hand, the jump ring is brought down to meet the solder join. The jump ring is held in position whilst the pallion melts, whereupon soldering is complete.

11

The pods are pickled, rinsed and dried thoroughly, then cleaned up with a Scotch-Brite™ pad.

12

A burnisher is used to create a bright edge on the rim of the pods.

13

A 'bar and loop' clasp is made for the fixing.

TIP Ground maize cob is a very useful drying medium. It absorbs moisture from hard-to-reach areas such as the insides of these pods. The pods are placed in the cob for five to ten minutes, and when removed they are completely dry.

Stringing on the beads
Tiger-tail wire can be used for
stringing. This material, made from
twisted steel wire coated in plastic, is
supple yet strong and ideally suited to
stringing gemstones.

A small section of specially purchased
silver tube, called a crimp, is used at
the ends to secure the wire. Specialised
pliers are used to close the crimps
firmly, and specialised cutters are used
to cut it. Silver beads are positioned
next to the crimp at both ends of the
bead strand.

Starting the bead-stringing by securing the first end of the bracelet
A jump ring is attached to both sections of the clasp. To start the bead-stringing
process, the tiger tail is fed through this jump ring and then both ends of the tail
are threaded through a silver bead and a crimp. The tiger tail is positioned so that
one end extends approximately 1 cm (0.394 in.) from the crimp. The crimp is
squeezed using the specialised pliers, which have two sections: the first is used to
flatten and curve the crimp onto the tiger tail, while the second section is used to
fold the crimp over to ensure a firm grip.

TIP The two strands of tiger tail must not cross inside the crimp when the
pliers are used to close it.

If the gemstone beads have a hole big enough to fit over both strands of the tail,
they can be threaded straight onto the tiger tail. Both sections of the tail are fitted
together inside the beads. If the end section of the 1 cm (0.394 in.) length tail
protrudes from the gemstone strand, it is snipped off using the cutters. If the holes
of the gemstones are too narrow for both sections of the tiger tail to fit through, an
extra silver bead is slotted next to the crimp over both strands and the remaining
1 cm (0.394 in.) tail is snipped off.

14
The gemstone beads are 3 mm (0.118 in.) diameter labradorite balls. Three stones
are placed as spacers between each silver pod.

> **TIP** A few extra stones can be added or removed from either end of the bracelet to obtain the required length. For symmetry's sake it is better to have an equal number of beads on both ends.

Securing the other end of the bracelet

Once all beads and pods are threaded on, a crimp and then a silver bead are threaded onto the end. The tail is then threaded through the jump ring on the other piece of the clasp. The tail is then brought back through the silver bead and crimp. If the gemstone bead holes are large enough, the tail is threaded through three or four beads going back up the bracelet. This ensures that an extra length of tiger tail exists at the end to give extra security. If the holes are too small, another silver bead is added before the crimp and the tail is threaded back up through the bead.

The tiger tail is pulled through the crimp and beads until all gaps between beads have been removed, ensuring that the tension on the tail is not too great; it is important to avoid the pods and beads looking too stiff on the strand. When the correct tension of the bracelet is achieved, the end is crimped off.

Finally, the remaining tiger tail is snipped off by placing the cutters close in to the bead strand, where it protrudes. Care is taken to ensure that the end of the tiger tail is snipped close to the bead so that none remains sticking out through the strand.

Multi-bell bracelet, *Rachel Dorris. Photo: Rachel Dorris.*

Rachel Dorris lives and works in London. Rachel retrained in jewellery-making in 2003 after leaving behind a career in medical physics. She exhibits at a variety of shows, sells her work through galleries and works to private commission. To view Rachel's work please visit www.racheldorris.co.uk.

Photography unless otherwise stated by John Hamilton Owen Smith.

The Multiple sphere bracelet *shown here, by Georgia Wiseman, (Scotland), further demonstrates the use of doming. The spheres are formed, hammered and soldered together. It is made in silver, oxidised, with an 18 ct gold catch. Photo: Georgia Wiseman.*

Double-felt Bangle *by Hannah Louise Lamb (Scotland) is made of silver and felt. The silver is roll-printed and fabricated with hand-pierced details and hand-dyed felt. Photo: Hannah Louise Lamb.*

This silver bangle by Mark Nuell (England) has been forged and wrapped, then overlaid with 22 ct gold. Photo: FXP.

Milky Way Cuff *by Nina Basharova (USA) is made from silver and has been cast, soldered and assembled. Photo: Jason Bolger.*

This piece, Carnivora #2 by Cristina Filgueira Dias (Sweden), is made from rubber, pigment, beads and plastic. Photo: Dean Powell.

3. Tap and die bangle with drilled stone by Melissa Hunt

INTRODUCTION

Tap and die sets are invaluable to a maker, especially one who wants to use a cold-fixing technique – securing materials that cannot necessarily withstand heat, or producing a piece of jewellery that can come apart, making it interchangeable. These tools can be fiddly to use, the correct dimensions of the apparatus being of the utmost importance; precision is imperative. This project has been designed to explain the technique as simply as possible.

For another useful cold-fixing technique see Lindsey Mann's project on riveting.

The final bangle in this project demonstrates perfectly the use of this equipment, using a drilled pebble as an example. The result is very effective.

TOOLS AND MATERIALS

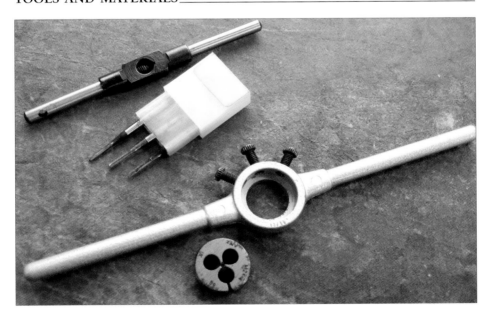

Specialist tools
- Set of three taps M2 x 0.4 to fit a 2 mm (0.079 in.) hole and tap wrench
- Die M2 x 0.4 to fit a 2 mm (0.079 in.) hole and die holder

Note: These dimensions have been taken directly from the tap and die set purchased from Clerkenwell Screws, to fit a 2 mm (0.079 in.) hole (see the list of suppliers at the end of the book for details).

Other tools and equipment
- Bench drill and 1.8 mm or 1.9 mm (0.071 in. or 0.075 in.) drill bits
- 2 mm (0.079 in.) diamond-tipped drill bit
- 3-in-1 oil (for lubrication)
- Fine emery paper
- Blu-Tack®
- Masking tape
- Basic jewellery tools and equipment

Materials
- 2.1 mm (0.083 in.) diameter, 18 ct hardened white-gold round wire
- 4 x 3 mm (0.157 x 0.118 in.) silver D-shaped wire bangle
- Pebble

HEALTH & SAFETY

Care must be taken when using the drill. Goggles must be worn and long hair tied back.

METHOD

1

A short taper is filed into one end of the 2.1 mm (0.083 in.) diameter, 18 ct hardened white-gold round wire. This will also remove any burrs. Do not anneal. This is known as the male part.

2

The wire is secured horizontally in a vice, and the die is screwed into the die holder. The wire is lubricated with 3 in 1 oil and the tip of the wire is aligned into the die. The die is then carefully turned clockwise to fit the wire in place to start cutting the thread. Pressure is evenly exerted on both handles, which are turned gently a quarter turn clockwise, occasionally reversing an eighth of a turn to eliminate swarf.

The female and male parts of the piece must be made of metals of different densities to prevent the thread from wearing away. In this project the bangle, the female part, is made from silver and the screw, the male part, is made from 18 ct hardened white-gold. The male part is 2.1 mm-diameter (0.083 in.) round wire especially drawn down in a draw plate. It must be slightly larger than the hole drilled into the female part.

3

The length of wire needed is threaded and cut with a piercing saw (see above image). It is then gently filed and fine emery is used to remove any burrs, with extreme care being taken not to damage the thread. A decorative piece can be soldered onto one end of the wire to make it into a screw – in this instance a cross shape. After soldering, the piece is pickled, cleaned up thoroughly, ensuring fire stain is removed from the cross, and then barrel-polished for at least ten minutes to work-harden it.

4

For the female part of the piece, the metal used must not be less than 3 mm (0.118 in.) thick, or enough to engage a distance of at least three revolutions. This prevents the screw from working itself loose whilst the jewellery is being worn. The female part of this project is a 4 x 3 mm (0.157 x 0.118 in.) D-shaped silver-wire bangle.

The bangle has been made as per the Basic Jewellery Techniques chapter, and a matt finish is then applied.

5

The bangle is held in a vice, a centre punch is used to mark where the hole is to be drilled and using a 1.8 mm or 1.9 mm (0.071 or 0.075 in.) drill bit, the hole is made avoiding any solder joins. A bench drill should be used to ensure a completely vertical hole.

6

The tap wrench is used to cut a thread into the hole using the three taps in succession according to their depth of cut, the shallowest cut first. It is lubricated with 3 in 1 oil and used in a slow, clockwise motion, with an occasional anticlockwise motion to eliminate swarf. These taps are hardened but still brittle, so the twist must not be forced because the tap could snap inside the piece of work.

TIP If unfortunately the tap does snap inside the metal, the piece should be immersed in safety pickle or alum overnight. This will gradually eat away the steel; the following day, if it is not totally dissolved it should at least be loose enough to be removed.

7

The pebble is positioned on some Blu-Tack® in a clear container and covered with water. A 2 mm (0.079 in.) diamond-tipped drill bit is drilled into the pebble slowly and gently. The water keeps the pebble and drill bit cool, preventing blunting. Masking tape can be put over the pebble if necessary to prevent the entrance or exit hole shattering.

8

Once the three parts are clean and ready, the piece of work is then assembled, ensuring that the screw mechanism does not extend past the inside edge of the piece. Should this happen, a file is used to shorten it.

Tap and die bangle with drilled stone, *Melissa Hunt.*

Melissa Hunt makes jewellery inspired by her surroundings: sea-worn glass and pebble pieces collected during her childhood on the South Coast led to a fascination with the effects of weathering, erosion and patinas, whilst studying at London Metropolitan University. Her exploration of jewellery-making techniques continues today at her London workshop, where she also produces a collection of men's jewellery featuring areas of the London A-Z.

Melissa lives and works in London and is a part-time tutor at the City Lit, London. Melissa exhibits and sells her work through galleries and shows, and can be contacted on melissahuntjewellery@hotmail.com.

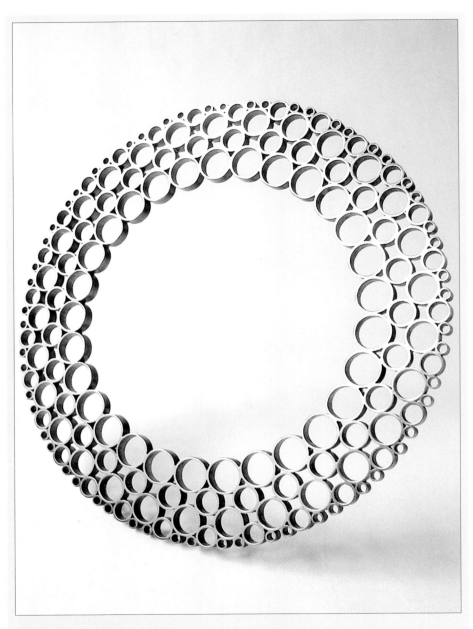

Chaos Bangle *by Sarah Stafford (England) is constructed from sections of silver tube which are individually soldered together. The piece is ground flat and polished, oxidised then burnished. Photo: Sarah Stafford.*

4. Knitted wire bangle
by Sarah Keay

INTRODUCTION

This project demonstrates how fine wire is cleverly knitted into a round tubular piece of jewellery simply using a bobbin and a crochet hook.

Sarah Keay uses this ancient technique of hand-bobbin knitting in her practice. She has adapted and developed the technique and cleverly combined the craft with contemporary materials and methods. The resulting long metal wire form looks fragile and yet it is much stronger than a woollen equivalent. The effect is stunning.

There are many ways in which a jeweller can work in wire. Please refer to *Wire Jewellery*, by Hans Stöfer, a handbook in this same A&C Black series.

TOOLS AND MATERIALS

Specialist tools
- A wooden eight-pegged bobbin. A four or six-pegged bobbin can also be used.
- Crochet hook.

Other tools and equipment
- Scissors or wire-cutters
- Round-nose pliers

Materials
- One reel of 0.5 mm (0.02 in.) enamelled wire (silver wire can also be used).
- Twenty or more plastic washers or curtain rings, available from any DIY store, haberdashery, ironmonger or craft shop. A selection of beads can also be used.

HEALTH & SAFETY

Care must be taken to work slowly so as to avoid accidents, especially to avoid the crochet needle slipping and to maintain control of the wire.

METHOD

1

The plastic washers are threaded onto the wire reel.

2

Holding the bobbin firmly with the thumb in front, the end of the wire is pushed down through the centre of the bobbin, leaving about three inches spare. The wire is wound anticlockwise around one of the pegs, then moved clockwise onto the next peg along. It is then wrapped anticlockwise around this next peg. Continuing in this manner until each peg has a loop around it. The wire must not be pulled too tight when knitting this first round, or it will make pulling the wire off the pegs in the next step very difficult.

> **TIP** If the wire is too thick it will be really difficult to use and uncomfortable to work, possibly leading to hand cramps. If the piece has to be stronger, layering different tubes across each other is recommended.

3

Once the wire has been wound around all of the pegs, the second row begins. The next loop is wound around the first peg, just above the existing loop, so there are now two loops around the one peg. Using a crochet hook, the bottom loop – the very first one made – is picked up and lifted up and over the new loop and completely off the peg. This procedure is continued onto the next peg – making a loop and then 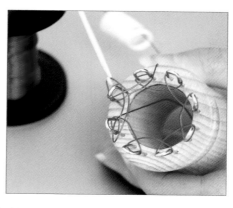 pulling the bottom loop over it and off the bobbin. This process continues, and soon a knitted tube emerges from the bottom.

4

Every few inches or so, a washer is dropped into the tube on the wire and knitting continues. The washer falls down the wire into the tube of knitting, as making continues the washer is knitted into place.

5

Knitting continues, dropping the washers in until the bangle reaches the desired length.

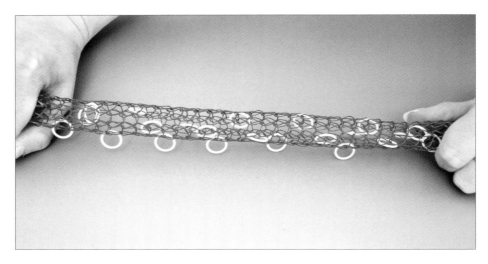

6
The bangle is gently pulled into shape by stretching the wire in between both hands.

7
To finish the bangle, all the loops are unhooked from the bobbin. The wire is cut from the reel using scissors or wire-cutters, depending on the hardness of the metal, leaving several inches at the end to work with. This extra wire is looped once through the last loop, to prevent it unravelling.

8
The wire is continually looped through each opposite loop until the ends are completely joined. The end is snipped off and round-nose pliers are used to tuck it in towards the middle of the tube so it does not scratch or catch on clothing.

The knitted bangle is now complete and ready to wear. Photo: K. Koppe, model: Tina Sullivan.

Since graduating from the Glasgow School of Art in 2003, Sarah Keay has taken part in numerous international group and solo exhibitions and has gained many prominent commissions. In 2006 she was awarded a startup grant from the Scottish Arts Council. Sarah has written a book for A&C Black Publishers in the *Design and Make* series, called *Jewellery Using Textile Techniques*. She lives and works in Dundee and can be contacted on sarahisobelkeay@hotmail.com.

Satellite Bracelet II, by Petra Bishia (England) is made of stainless-steel wire with silver and 18 ct gold melted, forged and embossed using rolling mills. The forged pieces are drilled and threaded onto the steel wire, and the ends are soldered. Photo: Jeremy Johns.

Dot Sim (Wales) has produced a sculptural 'roller bangle' made from oval silver wire, formed both on a mandrel and by hand. Photo: Victor Albrow.

Giovanni Corvaja (Italy) has produced this beautiful bracelet in 22 ct gold. He has developed a three-dimensional knitting technique that consists, in this case, of knitting one wire using 25 needles simultaneously. Photo: Giovanni Corvaja.

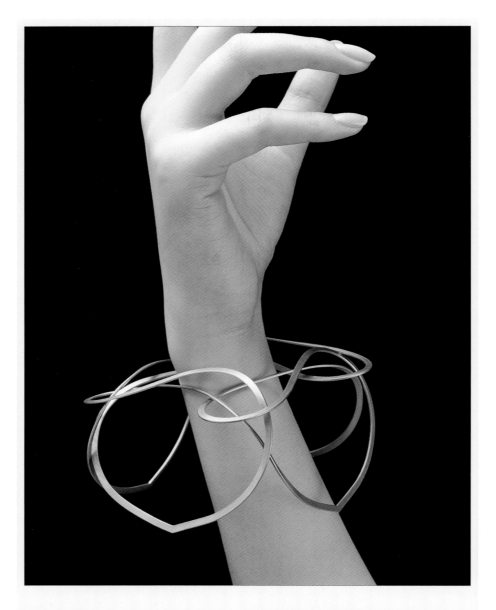

Elastic Gold 14, *a bangle by Hyunkyung Park (Korea), is the product of a project which focuses on the characteristics of metal, especially on structures that utilise 'elasticity'. It is made in 18 ct yellow gold. Photo: Studio Munch.*

5. Riveted aluminium layered bangle by Lindsey Mann

INTRODUCTION

This project demonstrates perfectly how riveting can be a very useful technique for creating a piece of jewellery with depth and form. Layers of metal are riveted together, revealing interior treasures and colours. Beads are also riveted to the outside of the bangle to give it additional decoration and dimension.

The project clearly describes how to make and use rivets, an important cold-fixing technique to use when soldering is either not possible or not desired. For another useful cold-fixing technique see Melissa Hunt's project on tap and die (page 49).

As is the hallmark of a piece of Lindsey Mann's work, this resulting bangle is stylish, colourful, quirky and beautifully made.

TOOLS AND MATERIALS

Tools (anticlockwise from left): heavy mallet, approximately 1 kg (2 lb), centre punch, chenier cutter, disc-cutter. Photo: Lindsey Mann.

Other tools and equipment
- Coarse-cut file (curved)
- Fine-cut files (flat and curved)
- Fine emery paper
- Emery sticks (flat and round)
- Small riveting hammer
- Drill and 1 mm (0.039 in.) drill bit
- Masking tape
- Accurate measuring device (for example, a Vernier gauge)
- Pencil
- Basic jewellery tools and equipment

Materials
- Pre-printed aluminium sheet 1 mm (0.039 in.) thick and approx. 100 x 200 mm (3.94 x 7.87 in.)
- Silver tubing 1 mm (0.039 in.) outside diameter
- Silver tubing 1 mm (0.039 in.) inside diameter – it must slot over the 1 mm (0.039 in.) outside diameter tubing
- Twelve beads with a hole size of 1 mm (0.039 in.) inside diameter

IMPORTANT TECHNICAL NOTE
Separate files, saw blades and emery paper must be used for aluminium work. Any aluminium dust that gets onto silver will create pitted marks when silver is heated. For this reason, these tools should be stored separately.

HEALTH & SAFETY

Care must be taken when using the drill. Goggles must be worn and long hair tied back. It is also recommended that a dust mask is worn if filing and finishing aluminium, especially when using emery or wet & dry paper.

METHOD

1
A template is made for the bangle by cutting a sheet of paper to a suitable shape. A bangle sizer is used to establish the correct size, drawing inside of the bangle sizer exactly onto the template. This section is then cut out with a scalpel knife. One

side of the template is marked with a cross to establish which side is which.

2

To mark out the two layers for the bangle; one side of the printed aluminium sheet is covered with masking tape. The template is placed over the sheet with the cross facing up, and drawn around using a pencil. The template is then turned over, moved along the masked aluminium sheet and drawn around again.

3

Saw blades are used to cut out the shapes, using a saw frame. A small drill is used to make a hole in the central sections, for feeding the blade through to cut the bangle holes. The inside of each bangle must be identical, something that is achieved using a coarse-cut file.

TIP The hole is drilled as close to the edge as possible, to avoid wastage. The cut-out circle can be used later for something else.

TIP Care is taken not to scratch the printed face of the sheets. Masking tape over the print can help, although not placed too close to the edge, as the glue on the tape sticks to the file and makes filing messy and difficult.

4

The masking tape is removed and all edges are cleaned using fine-cut files. A curved file is used for the inside and a flat file for the outside.

5
Fine emery paper is used to smooth out the edges; emery sticks are recommended for this – a flat stick for the outside edges and a round one for the inside edges.

6
A disc-cutter is used to punch three holes in a cluster on opposite ends of each of the bangle sheets. A heavy mallet is used to hammer the disc punch through the cutter. A triangular needle file is used to create a shaped edge, which is then cleaned up with emery paper.

7
The aluminium sheets are laid together and marked through onto the other sheet in the centre of the disc-cut hole. The centre is gently marked with a centre punch, and a 1 mm (0.039 in.) hole is drilled through each mark; each hole will hold a bead with a rivet on each side of the sheet.

8 *Making the rivets*
a) The heights of the beads to go on each side of the sheet are measured and the two measurements are added together. The 1 mm (0.039 in.) thickness of the sheet is added to this figure and an extra 1 mm (0.039 in.) to get the total.

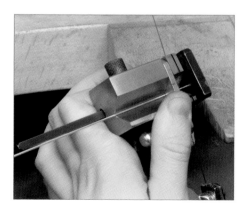

b) A chenier cutter is set to the total length and a length of silver tubing of 1 mm (0.039 in.) outside diameter is cut. The cut tube is fed through the drilled hole and a bead is fitted on each side of the sheet.

9 Closing the rivets

a) The stack is placed over a steel block with one bead facing down and one up.

A centre punch is placed into the top of the rivet and a small hammer is then gently tapped down onto the punch until the tube starts to flare.

b) The sheet is turned over and the process is repeated on the other side, working continually over a steel block, and gently hammering with a smooth-faced hammer directly onto the rivet to flatten it out. This process is repeated on the other side.

10

For each set of beads, stages 8 & 9 are repeated.

11

The two sections are placed together, and six or eight points around the bangle are marked to be drilled for rivets.

> **TIP** Four short lengths of 1 mm (0.039 in.) wire are cut to assist whilst drilling the rivet holes.

12

The two sheets are held together firmly, and one mark is drilled with a 1 mm (0.039 in.) drill bit. One of the 1 mm (0.039 in.) wires is used to plug the hole, the next mark is drilled, and that hole is again plugged. The holes are continued to be drilled, the wires will hold the two sheets securely and ensure that all the holes match up.

13

The chenier cutter is set at 3 mm (0.118 in.) and lengths of silver tubing of 1 mm (0.039 in.) inside diameter are cut, enough for each rivet. These will act as spacers, holding the two sheets apart.

14

The rivet lengths are established by adding the thickness of each sheet at 1 mm (0.039 in.) each, and the 3 mm (0.118 in.) for the spacer tubing and 1 mm (0.039 in.) extra, making a total of 6 mm (0.236 in.). The chenier cutter is then set at 6 mm (0.236 in.) and a length of 1 mm (0.039 in.) outside diameter is cut for each rivet hole.

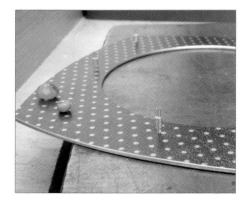

15

One sheet of the bangle is laid onto a steel block. A rivet tube is fitted into each hole and a spacer slotted onto the spacers as shown in the image adjacent.

The second sheet of bangle is fitted on top. A centre punch is used to open each rivet, turning the bangle over and repeating the process on the other side.

A smooth hammer is used to gently flatten each rivet on each side. When this is done, the bangle is complete.

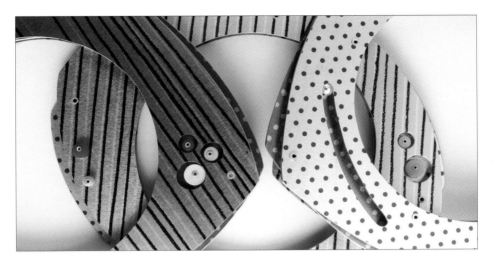

Lindsey Mann works intuitively, designing whilst making. By incorporating altered and found objects into jewellery she hopes to trigger the sensory memory of the viewer, creating foreign yet familiar associations.

Lindsey studied at Middlesex University, graduating in 2002. In 2005 she was awarded a Crafts Council Development Award. She works in Surrey, teaches jewellery-making and exhibits both nationally and internationally. Lindsey is currently writing a book in this A&C Black handbook series on coloured aluminium jewellery. Lindsey's work can be viewed at www.lindseymann.co.uk. She can be contacted at info@lindseymann.co.uk.

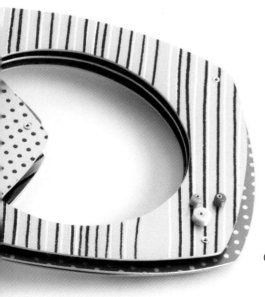

Examples of this bangle.
Photo: Joe Low.

69

Dainties Candies, *by Harriete Estel Berman (USA) is made from tin and plastic. The tin is cut with pinking shears, soldered and filled with plastic. The tin candies are attached with gold rivets. Photo: Philip Cohen.*

Overlap fold bangles *by Irene Metaxatos (USA). The fine silver sheet is mill rolled with pattern of seafan and wandering lines. It is then re annealed and folded either as overlap or to reveal a gold leaf seam. The edges are burnished. Photo: Irene Metaxatos.*

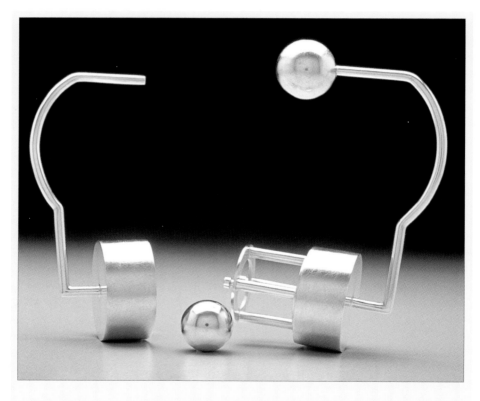

Caged sphere bracelet *by James Bové (USA), is a fabricated hollow constructed bracelet which contains a sterling silver sphere while being worn. The clasp allows the bracelet to break apart, freeing the sphere. Photo: David Smith.*

Mavi birthdays *by Lynda Watson (USA), is made using mixed materials.*
Photo: V. V. Jones.

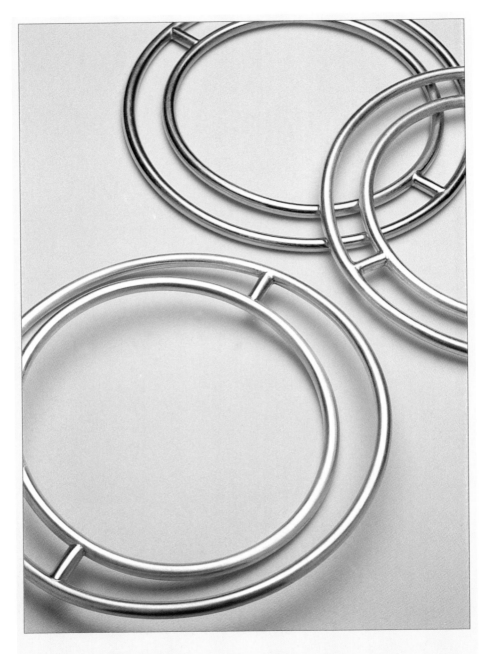

Noon Mitchellhill (England), has hand-fabricated these three bangles from silver wire, one of the bangles is gold plated. Photo: Joël Degen.

6. Hollow silver bangle by Jean Scott-Moncrieff

Made using the anticlastic raising technique, decorated with fused gold fragments

INTRODUCTION

This bangle is predominantly made using the anticlastic raising technique. Anticlastic raising is the term used when the jeweller/metalsmith 'compresses the centre of a sheet of metal and stretches its edges, forcing two sides to curl under and two sides to curve upward, resulting in the classic anticlastic form'. *www.professionaljeweler.com*

The bangle is made in two parts and then soldered together. The inner part of the bangle is raised on a stake, and a flat width of metal fused with gold is then soldered onto the outside.

The resulting bangle becomes a hollow form – a strong, bold and beautiful statement.

TOOLS AND MATERIALS

Specialist tools
Left to right: wooden oval bangle mandrel, flat-faced planishing hammer, curved-faced hammer, anticlastic raising stake, hard plastic-headed hammer with one end filed to a curve; large flat steel plate.

Other tools and equipment
- Wide flat file
- Large vice for the raising stake
- Large soldering area/fire bricks
- Large pickle pot
- Steel square
- Hand drill and 2 mm (0.079 in.) drill bit
- Blu-Tack®
- Basic jewellery tools and equipment

Materials
- Silver sheet 0.6 mm (0.024 in.) thick, 210 or 220 mm (about 8.27 in.) long x 38 mm (1.50 in.) wide
- Silver sheet 0.6 mm (0.024 in.) thick, 245 or 255 mm (about 9.65 in.) long x 40 mm (1.57 in.) wide
- 18 ct gold fragments (coarse filings, small pieces of wire, etc.)
- Hard solder

HEALTH AND SAFETY

Care must be taken when using the drill. Goggles must be worn and long hair tied back. Care must also be taken when piercing and soldering (please see the Basic Jewellery Techniques chapter for further details).

METHOD

Making the inner part

1
The short edges of a sheet of silver are filed straight (sheet dimensions: 0.6 mm (0.024 in.) thick, 210 or 220 mm (about 8.27 in.) long x 38 mm (1.50 in. wide). A steel square is used to ensure they are totally flat and at right angles to the long edges.

2

The sheet is annealed and curved round so that the short edges meet. The joint is kept together with two parallel pieces of binding wire, and hard solder is used on the outer surface to solder them together. The binding wire is removed, and the piece is then pickled, rinsed and dried.

3

The anticlastic raising stake is secured horizontally in a large vice. The annealed silver band is placed over the largest curve on an anticlastic raising stake. With a curved-faced hammer the silver is hit just in front of the point where it is in contact with the stake.

This hammering continues all the way round the band, then onto the other side. It is important that the hammer strikes the silver as evenly as possible, because these marks will show.

4

The band is annealed, pickled and rinsed and then pushed over a wooden oval bangle mandrel. The solder joint must be in the middle of one of the longer sides of the oval; the mandrel is marked with a permanent marker, to be used as a guide. The curved end of a hard plastic hammer is used to achieve the oval shape.

5

The edges are made true by using the flat end of the plastic hammer or a rawhide mallet on a flat plate.

Actions 3 to 5 are repeated, moving into a smaller curve of the anticlastic raising stake to achieve a tighter curve.

This image shows how as the curve gets deeper the width of the bangle gets narrower. If the solder joint starts to pull apart, it is soldered back together using binding wire to keep it tightly together during heating.

6

When the curve is right, the band is annealed again and placed on the outside of the high point of one of the curves of the anticlastic raising stake. The first set of hammer marks are smoothed out with a flat-faced planishing hammer.

Only the outer areas of the band can be planished before the edge of the face of the hammer will begin to catch on the inside curve. The edges of the curved inner band are filed straight. A steel square is used vertically on the flat plate while turning the silver band to check for any high spots. The high spots are marked carefully and filed away until both the outer edges are parallel with each other.

7

To establish the length of silver required for the outer part, a length of paper is wrapped around the edges and marked accurately where they overlap.

8

On the opposite side to the solder joint, the centre is marked and a 2 mm (0.079 in.) hole is drilled; this is to allow for the expansion of air inside, which will heat up when the two parts are soldered together.

Making the outer part

9

The sheet of silver metal is annealed, pickled and flattened. Sheet dimensions: 0.6 mm (0.024 in.) thick, 245mm or 255 mm (about 9.65 in.) long x 40 mm (1.57 in.) wide. A rawhide mallet is used to flatten the metal on the flat plate.

The silver sheet can be decorated in many ways: by roller-pressing, etching, planishing, rough hammering, or leaving it plain to be polished later. This bangle has had 18 ct gold fragments fused onto the outer surface.

Fusing onto the outer surface

10

The length of silver is fully supported on fire bricks in a large soldering area. It is then annealed and pickled five times until a good layer of fine silver has come to the surface – manifesting as an opaque white 'bloom' on the silver.

This process is important because the fine silver is purer than the rest of the sterling alloy and has a slightly lower melting point than the centre of the sheet. This means that it will melt fractionally earlier, so with very careful use of the flame one can achieve reticulation and fusing without melting through the whole sheet.

11

A thin layer of milky borax is painted onto the silver and a thick layer of gold fragments are sprinkled in a stripe, avoiding the long edges. A dry brush is used to push the gold into a fairly even layer. The piece is then warmed up slowly by the flame so that the borax does not dry too quickly and spit the gold off the surface of the silver. The heat is increased carefully, and the surface begins to reticulate as the gold is fused into it.

> **TIP** It is not always necessary to use new gold when fusing, in this instance the gold fragments consist of coarse filings, small pieces of wire and scrap metal.

> **TIP** Great care must be taken not to melt the edges of the silver; the flame must be kept moving along the central area all the time. If flashes of 'wet' areas show on the surface of the silver, the flame should immediately be moved away or a hole will appear in the metal.

12

When the whole length is fused, the sheet is carefully placed, as flat as possible, into the pickle. It is then rinsed very gently and left to dry under a lamp. The fused surface must not be patted dry with a cloth, because if some of the gold has not yet adhered to the silver, it will come off.

13

When the length is absolutely dry, it is placed on a large piece of tissue paper on the flat plate. A flat-faced planishing hammer is used to planish the entire surface of the silver, forcing the fused gold further into the surface. Any pieces of gold that come off can be saved in the tissue paper and used again. If any areas have lost their gold fragments, the fusing process is repeated again until fully satisfied with the decoration.

Note: After the outer part has been soldered to the inner curved part, it is not possible to do any more fusing.

Putting the two parts together

14

The length of the outer part is checked using the paper that was wrapped around the inner curved part. The short edges are filed flat, using a steel square to ensure they are at right angles to the long edges. The metal is then annealed and curved up so that the short edges meet. The joint is kept together with two parallel pieces of binding wire, and hard solder is used on the inside.

The binding wire is then removed and the piece is pickled, rinsed and dried.

15

The band is pushed over the oval bangle mandrel, and a rawhide mallet is used to true up the shape, ensuring that the solder joint is in the middle of one of the longer sides of the oval.

16

The inner curved part is put onto the flat plate, and the outer part is pushed over, making sure the soldered edges match up.

TIP Beeswax is rubbed along the edges of the inner part to help it move smoothly down inside the outer part.

The edges of the outer part must be standing proud of the inner part on both sides so that the inner part is centrally placed. The inner edges need to be a tight fit with the outer part to ensure a good solder joint.

17
The top inside-edge joint is coated in borax, and large pallions of hard solder are placed along the joint, in an upright position, supported by the outer edge.

The joint is then soldered and allowed to cool, then pickled, rinsed and dried. Then the soldering is repeated on the other side.

TIP Cooling slowly will lessen any twisting or distortion.

18
When the piece is cool, before placing it in the pickle, the small drilled hole is carefully covered with a small piece of Blu-Tack to avoid the pickle seeping in. Once complete, the water is shaken out and the piece is left to dry out completely in a warm place.

TIP If pickle seeps into the hole, the entire piece will need to be boiled in water with soda crystals to neutralise the pickle.

19

When both sides have been successfully soldered and all the pickle removed, the excess part of the outer edge is pierced away.

20

The edges are filed, and any excess solder that may have run down onto the inner curved part is removed with a file. The edges and curved inside part of the piece are finished with finer and finer gradations of wet & dry papers.

21

Finally, the edges are burnished and the bangle is complete.

The finished bangle. Photo: FXP.

Hollow Silver Bangle

Jean Scott-Moncrieff works in London and Sussex and is a regular exhibitor at the prestigious Goldsmiths' Fair. She works mainly to commission and produces small editions for galleries. Some of her work can be seen at www.jeanscott-moncrieff.co.uk.

Michael Carberry (England), perfectly demonstrates how to forge fine silver into handmade bangles. Photo: Joël Degen.

Umut Demirguc (Turkey) has formed a bangle from sterling silver. The Ottoman Empire motifs are pierced into the sheet before the bangle is soldered together. Photo: Umut Demirguc.

Jill Newbrook (England) has fabricated a bangle using silver sheet with mokume gane *inserts. The* mokume gane *is made of mixed layers of copper, silver and Japanese shakudo and shibuichi. The two curved sections are formed on a mandrel and soldered to each edge, and a band is then soldered to the inside. Photo: Joël Degen.*

This bangle by Kathie Murphy (England), is made of polyester resin and thread cast into a silicone rubber mould in two parts. Polyester resin is a liquid plastic which is turned solid by the addition of a catalyst. This triggers an exothermic reaction, which sets the plastic and cannot be reversed. The inside of the bangle is pale blue and is the first pouring. Once this is set the second pour is made over the green thread. Kathie says 'The delight for me is that although I can control where the thread goes in the bangle, there is always an element of surprise when the resin moves the threads slightly as it is poured in, giving rise to some delightful results'. The shape of the bangle also enhances the play of light and colour through the piece. Photo: Kathie Murphy.

7. Anodised aluminium and silver charm bracelet
by John Moore

INTRODUCTION

This charm bracelet, by John Moore, is a signature piece in the Elytra collection, combining silver with dyed, anodised aluminium. Multiple charms arranged in gradually changing rainbow colours move freely when the bracelet is worn to create a delicate noise.

Due to the success of the Elytra range, John has developed specialist equipment and processes for cutting, finishing and forming the charms on this bracelet, where previously he had made them using hand tools.

TOOLS AND MATERIALS

(1)fly press fitted with a special punch, made to specifications; (2)urethane rubber block and acrylic former; (3)micro-motor; (4)pin vice and ball burr; (5)RT blanking tool; (6)sprung parallel pliers; (7)snipe-nose pliers.

Other tools and equipment

- Split pin fitted with 400-grade wet & dry paper
- Basic jewellery tools and equipment

Materials
- Sheet of dyed, anodised aluminium 0.5 mm (0.02 in.) thick and about 165 x 125 mm (6.50 x 4.92 in.)
- Silver sheet for the bar about 0.5 mm (0.02 in.) thick
- Silver round wire for the loop 1.5 mm (0.059 in.) in diameter, about 28 mm (1.10 in.) long)
- Silver jump rings 0.5 mm (about 0.02 in.) diameter, made of 0.9 mm (0.035 in.) round wire
- Length of silver chain, about 180 mm (7.09 in.)

Important technical note: Separate files, saw blades and emery paper are used for aluminium work. Any aluminium dust that gets onto silver will create pitted marks when silver is heated. These tools should be stored separately.

HEALTH AND SAFETY

When using a fly press great care must be taken to avoid accidents. It is a very heavy piece of equipment and must be used with caution. Safety goggles must be worn when drilling, using a micro-motor or a pendant motor, and long hair must be tied back. It is recommended that a dust mask is worn if filing and finishing aluminium, especially when using emery or wet & dry paper.

METHOD

1
A sheet of dyed, anodised aluminium, 0.5 mm (0.02 in.) thick and about 165 x 125 mm (6.50 x 4.92 in.) is chosen to make the charms. The metal has been carefully dip-dyed to achieve a subtle graduation of rainbow colours.

2
The sheet is cut lengthways into strips to achieve a colour gradation.

3

The charms are stamped out by feeding strips of material through a special punch using a fly press shown here. Alternatively, shapes can be cut out using the RT blanking system (see the Glossary at the end of the book and stage 7 below) or marked with a stencil and cut out using a piercing saw.

> **TIP** Using a pencil to make marks on aluminium does not damage the coloured surface; they can be rubbed off easily afterwards. Marking the metal with a scriber, must be avoided as any scratches cannot be removed.

4

In this instance the special punch has been designed specifically to make a 1.2 mm (0.04 in.) hole at one end of each charm, but these can also be marked out by hand using a centre punch then drilled through. The middle image shows the various stages of production.

5

The edges of each charm are finished using 400-grade wet & dry paper in a split pin on a micro-motor. A micro-motor is similar to a pendant motor, only more sensitive. After smoothing the edges with the tool held at 90°, any metal burrs are gently removed by holding the tool at 45°. Alternatively, wet & dry paper on a flat stick can be used. Great care must be taken to avoid marking the anodised surface.

TIP If the pieces are too small to hold between fingers, a pair of sprung parallel pliers are used, lined with a double layer of masking tape to avoid marking the surface.

6

A ball burr gripped into a pin vice is used to remove any burrs, or alternatively a slightly larger drill bit. A few gentle turns on each side of the hole will remove burrs without damaging the surface of the metal.

7

An RT blanking tool in the fly press is used to make the 'bar' of the bar-and-hoop catch, the shape being a larger version of the charm. The tool is sandwiched between two sheets of Kevlar or steel, while the silver sheet is 0.5 mm (0 .02 in.) thick. Alternatively, the shape can be pierced out with a saw blade. The edges are finished using a file, then wet & dry paper.

A small round ring is made from a length of silver wire to form the hoop, making sure it is just large enough for the bar to pass through, but not so large that it will fall through easily.

8

Each charm is curved using an acrylic former attached to the ram of the fly press and a block of urethane rubber. The former has been carved by hand, but a doming punch can also be used for this purpose, remembering that this might mark the aluminium.

TIP Urethane rubber, as opposed to using a solid material for the female part of a mould, will wrap the metal around any male former while maintaining the surface finish. The former must always be clean of particles that might dent the surface.

9

The same process is repeated with the silver catch before a small U-shaped piece of wire is soldered to the centre of the back.

10

The bar and hoop are attached to either end of a length of silver chain using jump rings which are then soldered closed.

TIP Solder paste is recommended for soldering jump rings, as soldering with pallions can be very tedious when they keep falling off.

11

The bar and hoop are then pickled, rinsed and dried. If necessary, at this point the chain is run through the barrel polisher for 10 minutes to bring the chain back up to a high shine.

12

The bracelet is then assembled using silver jump rings of 5 mm (0.197 in.) diameter, made of 0.9 mm (0.035 in.) thick wire. This is done by hanging the chain from a hook attached to the edge of a bench. Jump rings are opened with a twisting motion using parallel pliers in each hand.

Six charms are attached to every other link in the chain, three on either side. These jump rings are not soldered because the aluminium will melt. The charms are then rearranged into their original order so that the colour will change gradually in the finished bracelet.

The finished bracelet. Photo: John Moore.

John Moore has been designing and making jewellery since graduating from Manchester Metropolitan University in 2002. Inspired by Amazonian artefacts and natural forms, his distinctive designs in brightly coloured anodised aluminium continue to evolve and can be found in reputable galleries across the UK. In 2008 the British Jewellers' Association presented him with first prize in the Kayman Award for his Vane collection. For further information visit www.johnmoorejewellery.com.

Miranda Sharp (England) demonstrates a charm-style bracelet made in silver and resin. Some of the components are cast, while texture is applied via the roll mill, and pink resin is applied to other components. The piece is built up with a variety of charms that move beautifully on the wrist. Photo: Stephen Lenthall.

Here Tone Vigeland (Norway) demonstrates the beauty of multiple components by connecting the silver elements to silver mesh, each element having been made by hand. Collection: National Museum of Decorative Art, Trondheim, Norway. Photo: Hans-Jørgen Abel.

Blossom Bud Cluster, *Donna Barry (Edinburgh)*, an oxidised silver and 18 ct gold bracelet. The budlike elements have been blackened and rubbed back, revealing different surface patterns and textures. They are threaded onto a flexible steel wire, with the buds naturally grouping into clusters. Photo: Donna Barry.

This Multiple random *bangle by Amanda Doughty (England) is made in silver and 18 ct gold. Two of the bangles are made of silver and 18 ct gold metal which is fused together. One shows the gold on the outside and the other on the inside, the remaining bangles are entirely silver. Photo: Jeremy Johns.*

8. Fabricated Multiple Bangle with moving element by Amanda Doughty

Made using the wax carving technique

INTRODUCTION

This project demonstrates how to make a silver multiple bangle with an element. The element moves freely around a stack of bangles, and the bangles themselves are fabricated from rectangular silver wire, the making of which is demonstrated fully in the Basic Jewellery Techniques chapter. The element is carved from wax, a process described in detail here, and the wax is then cast into silver using the lost-wax casting technique. This latter task I entrust to a company specialising in the field, in this instance Quality Castings based in London, UK (see the list of suppliers at the end of the book for details). Finally, the two different aspects of the piece are brought together.

Not every jewellery workshop has casting equipment. Using a company to cast wax models (or metal masters) opens up design possibilities that might not previously have been achievable. Before embarking on production it is important to understand the key principles and limitations of this technique.

Wax carving, in jewellery terms, is the cutting of wax with a variety of sharp instruments to create a desired form or design, sometimes a form that might not have been achievable if fabricated in metal. This wax form can then be cast in the required metal.

*The photograph shows a bangle similar to the one described in this chapter.
Photo: Jeremy Johns.*

97

TOOLS AND MATERIALS

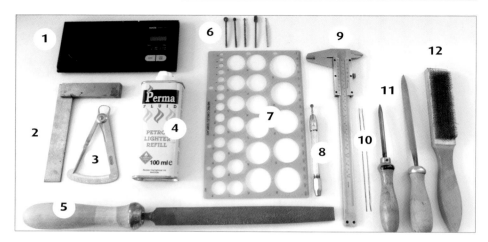

Specialist tools (above)

1 Accurate weighing scales, to weigh down to 0.1 g
2 Steel square
3 Tenth gauge
4 Lighter fuel/white spirit and soft cotton cloth (soft cloth not pictured)
5 A large coarse file just for wax carving
6 Wax-carving burrs and drills bits – old blunt setting burrs are best
7 Circle template
8 Pin vice fitted with a burr to hand-carve the wax
9 Vernier gauge
10 Wax-cutting saw blades
11 Two scrapers (two sizes shown here)
12 Steel brush to remove wax waste from files

Other useful tools and equipment for wax carving (opposite)

1 Wax pen – Max Wax (available from Cooksons)
2 Alcohol lamp for soft flame
3 Oval template
4 Large needle
5 Scalpel with a triangular blade fitted
6 Wax-carving tools or dental tools
7 Coarse smaller files purchased from cheap high-street tool shops
8 Wax needle file

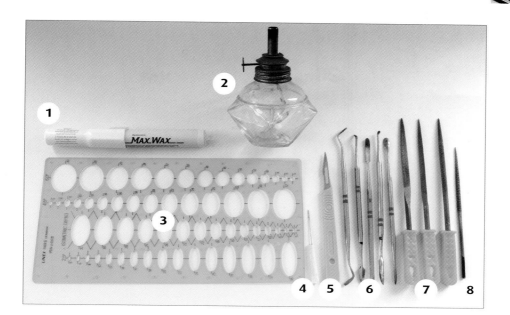

Other tools
• Basic jewellery tools and equipment
• Ring sizer stick

Materials
• Length of green ring wax tube
• Eight silver bangles of slightly varying diameters but equal thickness and width 0.84 mm (0.033 in.) thick and 6 mm (0.236 in.) wide, completed up to stage 9 in the Basic Jewellery Techniques chapter.

HEALTH AND SAFETY

Care must be taken when using the scalpel and sharp tools necessary for wax carving. Care must also be taken when using the pendant motor and attachments. Goggles must be worn and long hair must be tied back.

WAX TYPES

The wax is available as a block, as slices, ring tubes, wire and sheet. Its colour denotes its level of hardness: soft, medium, hard and very hard. Soft wax is pink and pliable: it can be folded, twisted, stamped, textured or built up into a texture. Medium wax is blue and is said to be the most versatile to carve and retain its shape. Hard wax is green and is slightly harder to work but good to use to create a good sharp form. Very hard wax is red and harder than the other three waxes.

When making a wax model it is generally not recommended that different wax types are combined together; they have different melting points and thus are quite often difficult for the caster to cast successfully.

METHOD

Carving a wax element from a ring-tube wax

When making a wax model it is important to note that the final metal casting will have shrunk by approximately 7 to 10% during the casting process. It is very difficult to establish what the exact amount of shrinkage will be, as it depends on the size and shape of the model or pattern. If the item is a ring, it will be approximately one and a half ring sizes smaller.

1

A section of wax tubing is cut to the required width using a wax blade fitted into a saw frame. To ensure a straight line, the wax is scored evenly all the way round the outside of the tube with a pair of dividers prior to piercing. During piercing, the wax tube is turned at intervals to ensure an even cut. The blade is a spiral shape so that the wax does not clog it up.

2

A coarse file is used to clean up the wax and make it accurate and straight on both of the flat sides.

A steel square is ideal for neatening up: scraping it across the wax will remove excess wax and flatten the surface.

3

It is important initially to establish the

100

inside measurement before working on the outside of the wax. This is especially important if the piece is going to be a ring. A very efficient method of establishing how much wax to carve away is to use a ring sizer, a vernier gauge and a pair of dividers.

a) The vernier gauge jaws are fitted around the required size on a ring stick sizer. British ring size 'M' / American ring size just under 6½ in this instance is 16.79 mm (0.661 in.).

b) The gauge is tightened into place by the screw, so that it is held in position.

c) The jaws of the gauge, which sit on the top of the device, narrow individually to points and accurately measure the inside of objects. This is the same measurement of

16.79 mm (0.661 in.) from the gauge jaws which are fitted around the ring stick sizer. Using the pointed jaws, the measurements can be scored onto the wax across the wax hole in two or more places.

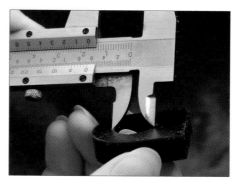

d) Dividers are set at the correct distance to the score lines and marked evenly around the hole, on the front and the back of the wax.

As a less involved alternative method to the above, a metal ruler can be marked at 16mm (0.63 in.), placed evenly over the wax hole, and the additional size scored on either side. Then follow stage 3d above.

4

Using a scraper, the inside of the hole is cut away at an angle up to the scored line, thus ensuring it is both round and the required size. Using long clean strokes, the remaining inside wax is then removed with the scraper. The wax size is checked on the ring stick sizer, care is taken not to remove too much wax.

TIP A ring wax cutter is much quicker and can be used for stages 3 and 4: a ring sizer with a sharp knife edge, it makes a concentric cut when turned around the interior of the wax.

5

The required design is marked out with dividers and a scriber and circular template. By marking out the design and using it as a guide, there is much better control over the carving, rather like a sculptor carving a piece from stone. Of course, working freehand without marking out will let the form evolve naturally. Both approaches have their merits.

The beauty of working in wax is that not only is it quick, it is also relatively inexpensive to use and experiment with. A wide variety of textures and finishes can be produced using these tools. Experimenting is the key to developing and mastering this technique. Wax carving is ideal for creating forms that would usually be difficult to obtain if fabricated from metal.

6

The surplus wax around the outer edge is pierced away, and the remaining shape is straightened up with a file and the steel square.

7

The element can now begin to be shaped and formed using a variety of wax-carving hand tools, the scraper and the burrs on the pendant motor. A ball burr is used to recreate a hollow form on the outside of the element.

The finished silver element must not be too heavy, or it will make the bangle uncomfortable and impractical to wear.

It is possible to make a wax form hollow, creating a bold piece without the weight. This is done by hollowing out the inside of the chosen design with a wax-carving ball burr (hollowing out the inside of this element is not appropriate in this instance). Great care must be taken when doing this; the wall thickness of any part of the wax should never be less than 1 mm (0.039 in.), as this would make casting more precarious. The thickness of the wax wall is measured with a tenth gauge.

> **TIP** A wax reamer is a tool that makes perfect wax blanks. Whilst it does not create unique and original masters, the blanks could be a base on which to work.

8
The wax is weighed regularly on accurate scales in order to estimate its metal weight for suitability for wearing (see the chart on pages 106-7 for conversion equations).

Wax repair
The surrounding broken area must be melted before the mend will fuse, and the centre of the break must be mended. The two pieces are gently melted around the broken area and held together until fixed into place. A Max Wax pen is very useful for repairing damaged waxes and filling in small areas. Wax pens are also ideal for building up areas and creating interesting textured surfaces. Small wax filings carved from the model are melted on the tip of the wax pen until they form a ball, which can then be reapplied to the piece.

9
Various tools are used to create as smooth a finish as possible, a scraper being ideal. A smooth surface can also be achieved using emery papers, although these can sometimes be messy. The better the finish on the wax model, the less finishing work there is to do when it is cast in metal.

10
Finally, the wax is polished with a soft cotton cloth and lighter fuel or white spirit. The finished wax needs a sprue, which in lost-wax-casting terms means the tube down which the molten metal will flow. The casting company will almost always add the sprue, as they have invaluable experience of where best to place it, thus avoiding the disappointment of a possible faulty casting.

11
This wax model is sent to Quality Castings to be cast in silver for a one-off casting. The casting company will take at least a week to complete the casting. Timings vary according to production timetables and holiday periods.

From left to right, this image shows the element in its three stages: the wax model, the raw silver cast and the finished cast with gold plating.

One-off casting using the lost-wax process

Though it has been refined over time, the lost-wax process is an ancient technique whose principle remains fundamentally the same. Essentially, this is the process whereby a form is first modelled in wax, then a casting process is used in which the wax model is melted or 'lost', to create a void within the cast that can then be filled with molten metal. The means that a finished wax can be cast once into metal without the need to make a mould. This is called a one-off casting process and is the technique used in this project.

Multiple casting

If multiple metal castings are required, a cold-cure silicon mould (which will then be used to produce multiple wax castings, using the lost wax process) can be produced directly from the wax. This is recommended only if the wax model is absolutely correct. Alternatively, the finished wax can be cast as a one-off and when returned, the piece is approved for production and cleaned up to a high standard, and any file marks, casting holes, seams or imperfections are removed. This then becomes the metal master for a vulcanised rubber mould. It is not possible to use a vaulcanised rubber mould directly with the original wax model because wax is fragile and the making of a vulcanised rubber mould uses pressure and heat.

Important note

It is important to understand what is possible and impossible in mould making terms when embarking on making a master that you intend on becoming a piece that is cast many times. There are some designs that simply can not be produced from one rubber mould – for example a hollow bead. There is no way to free the rubber inside the bead, assuming that the rubber could even get in there in the first place. The resulting piece that would be produced from this attempt would be a solid bead, not a hollow one. To produce a hollow bead, the bead must be presented to the caster in two halves and moulds made of them both (if the two halves are identical, one mould only needs to be made), the halves can then be soldered together once cast in metal.

Masters that have severe undercuts in their design cannot be released from a rubber mould without some distortion and so they should be avoided altogether. For example a small dish shape with a very steep lip would prove very hard to remove from the mould without having to destroy it. This type of design must be avoided, unless the intention is for it only to be a one off casting, using the lost wax process, where no mould making is necessary.

Vulcanised rubber moulds and cold-cure silicon moulds

Vulcanised rubber moulds use pressure and heat and thus are suitable for hard metal models, not wax or fragile objects. Cold-cure silicon moulds enable a variety of fragile objects to be cast – for example, wax, plastic, organic materials such as leaves, twigs, flowers, a fly, a bee and so on. Silicon also has a lower shrinkage performance. The main disadvantage is its higher cost and shorter working life when compared to vulcanised rubber moulds.

There are also 'non-shrink' and 'titanium' moulds available which are also said to reduce shrinkage. It is always best to consult with the casting company before investing too much time and money in model-making without the assurance that casting the work is viable.

Platinum is cast using a different casting technique altogether, which involves centrifugal casting.

To determine the weight of the finished metal piece and to estimate the price, specific to one-off, lost-wax casting

a) Multiply the weight of the wax model by the specific gravity of the metal to be cast. (See the two charts – Specific Gravity of Precious Metals and Weight Conversion Chart – at the end of this project for converting wax and metal models.)
b) Multiply this figure by the cost of the metal to be cast (price on application to the casting company). This will be priced per gram and is usually a little dearer than bullion prices.

c) Add the one-off casting fee (again price on application to the casting company, as it depends on the volume of the wax).
d) Finally, add VAT.

It is very difficult to estimate the cost of having a mould made, as this will vary according to how big the mould needs to be. There are of course practical limitations on the size of the piece, as this type of casting is small-scale. The largest volume of wax that could fit into the largest flask used for casting is approximately 12 cm (4.724 in.) wide by 4.5 cm (1.772 in.) deep, it is advisable to consult with the casters before commiting to the work. Jewellers usually send their waxes very carefully wrapped in the post, though some prefer to hand-deliver. Making an appointment to visit the casting company in person enables a client to discuss the specifics of their particular job, including prices and timescales.

Whilst the casting process is a very reliable one, casting companies can never guarantee that the casting will be a complete success. Occasionally, though rarely, for various reasons a wax casting will not succeed. By having a cold cure mould made of the wax model initially it minimises the risk of disappointment.

Specific gravity of precious metals

24 ct gold (pure gold)	19.36
18 ct yellow gold	15.58
Platinum	21.45
Silver	10.53
Sterling silver	10.40
Copper	8.94

Quality Castings' weight conversions based on identical volumes

From	To	Sum	Calculation
Wax	Silver	x	10
Wax	9 ct yellow gold	x	12
Wax	9 ct white gold	x	13
Wax	9 ct red gold	x	13
Wax	18 ct yellow gold	x	16
Wax	18 ct white gold	x	16.5

Wax	Bronze	x	8
Wax	Platinum	x	22.5
Silver	9 ct yellow gold	x	1.1
Silver	18 ct white gold	x	1.65
9 ct yellow gold	9 ct white gold	x	1.1
9 ct yellow gold	18 ct gold	x	1.4
9 ct yellow gold	Platinum	x	2.1
14 ct gold	9 ct yellow gold	x	0.815
18 ct gold	Platinum	x	1.5
18 ct white gold	9 ct yellow gold	x	0.688
Pewter	9 ct gold	x	1.6
Copper	9 ct yellow gold	x	1.3
Bronze	9 ct yellow gold	x	1.38
Steel	18 ct gold	x	1.875

These charts are very helpful to a jeweller who is making waxes or metal masters, and also for quoting a client the cost of a piece of jewellery in a different metal if it already exists in one kind of metal. They make it very easy to calculate the weight of a particular piece in another material and therefore to estimate that piece's final weight and approximate cost. These figures have been rounded up or down very slightly to make calculating a little easier.

Putting the bangles and the element together

The eight silver bangles have been completed up to stage 9 in the Basic Jewellery Techniques chapter. At this point the edges are also flattened and cleaned up; if left until later it becomes more awkward to do this accurately, especially if a disc sander is being used.

The element has been cast in silver; the remaining sprue is pierced off, and the entire casting is filed and thoroughly cleaned up, ensuring all the fire stain has been removed. Gold plating is applied, this being easier to do at this stage, before the element is in place.

The remaining metal sprue returned on the casting should be kept. When there are enough metal sprues collected from various jobs to warrant special delivery postage, they can be returned in exchange for a bullion price usually credited to your account.

12

The eight silver bangles are cut open and the element is slotted onto each bangle.

13

Each of the eight bangles are then soldered back together. Soldering is carefully done, with each bangle being set up separately so as to avoid as much as possible heating up the other bangles and the element. Heat bricks are strategically placed in front of the rest of the bangles, and the gold plating on the element is protected with a heat protector such as cool paste. Manipulating each individual bangle into place means the joins to be soldered are held tightly together without the need for binding wire to secure them. If the bangles resist tight positioning, each bangle is annealed, pickled then dried. This relieves any tension in the metal and allows the joins to sit tight for soldering.

TIP Initially coating each of the eight solder joins with borax prior to any soldering avoids the need to pickle the entire bracelet every time heat is applied. The bracelet is allowed to cool down before the next bangle is positioned carefully on the bricks with solder pallions tightly set in between the join.

14

The entire bangle is left to cool and then pickled, rinsed and dried.

15

The bangle is then completed as per the Basic Jewellery Techniques chapter, from stage 9 onwards. The cast silver element is always carefully held away from the bangle mandrel, the flatting press and polishing motor, to ensure that it is not damaged and does not distort the eight bangles in any way.

16

A polished finish is applied to the bangle and then is placed in the barrel polisher for one hour, this will not damage the gold plating. Once this is done, a matt finish is then applied to unplated areas of the element with the use of a matting block, as seen in the basic techniques chapter The bangle is then complete.

This Thorn bangle *by Chris Hawkins (England) is made in silver with a satin finish. The original carving has been made using the lost-wax casting process. Photo: Splitimage Design, Mark Curtis.*

Emma Farquharson (England), has produced her Loop-link bracelet *from cast silver links. These are assembled and soldered. Photo: Ralph Gabriner.*

Here Catherine Hills's (England) Ladybug bracelet *demonstrates perfectly the success of casting multiple elements and creating a charmlike effect. The entire bracelet is made in silver, and the elements are oxidised. Photo: Patrick Harrison.*

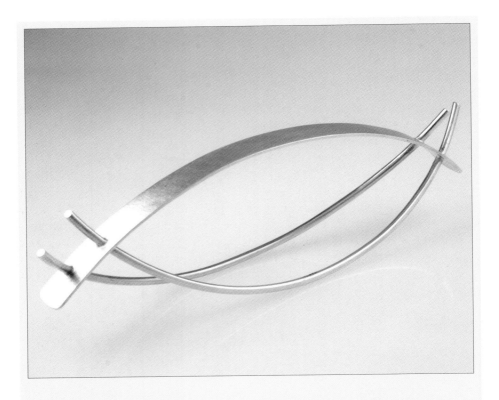

Lozenge bangle with gauze texture, *by Gill Newton (England). This bangle is fabricated from silver sheet and wire. The sheet has a cotton gauze and watercolour paper-shaped, roll-textured finish. Photo: Rob Popper.*

Conclusion

During my research for this book, it has become clear to me just how many ways there are to approach making jewellery, be it using an ancient technique or up-to-the-minute technology and machinery.

It has been especially fascinating to discover a great wealth of makers and to view the amazing work that goes on in workshops across the globe. Each jeweller designs and makes jewellery, either for a pursuit of pleasure or running a business, making jewellery for a living. This book focuses on the design and creation of bangles and bracelets.

Each of us strive to be original, to work towards the unique, trying to design what we consider to be fresh and new. This is paramount in the jewellery world. Why make a piece that we know already exists; why not instead try continually to push the boundaries? This is clearly easier said than done, but let's hope that the work generously shared by the contributors in this book will inspire and encourage us all to move forward, continually developing our own ideas.

Mitosis and Sponge Spine Forms *by Evan H. Larson (USA). This bangle is made of copper and has been fold-formed: the copper is folded in half, pierced out, filled, sanded and then annealed. The cells are hammered onto the folded spine. The cells are also etched. The piece has a heat patina made from cupric nitrate. Photo: R.H. Hensleigh.*

Suppliers

The list below is only a selection of suppliers available; it has been compiled from the recommendations of the jewellers included in this book. There are, of course, many other companies to choose from. Please note, they are suppliers to the trade.

UK TOOL SUPPLIERS AND BULLION DEALERS

Some of the suppliers below might also be refiners; contact them directly for further details.

Bellore (also supplies beads)
39 Greville Street
Hatton Garden, London
EC1N 8PJ
Telephone: +44 (0)20 7404 3220
Fax: +44 (0)20 7404 3221
order@bellore.co.uk
www.bellore.co.uk

Michael Bloomstein Precious Metals
30 Gloucester Road
Brighton, East Sussex
BN1 4AQ
Telephone: +44 (0)1273 608374
Fax: +44 (0)1273 690788
enquiries@bloomsteins.co.uk
www.bloomsteins.co.uk

Cookson Precious Metals/Exchange Findings
Birmingham branch (head office)
59-83 Vittoria Street
Birmingham B1 3NZ
Telephone: +44 (0)845 100 1122 or +44 (0)121 200 2120
Fax: +44 (0)121 212 6456
birmingham.sales@cooksongold.com
www.cooksongold.com

London branch
49 Hatton Garden
London
EC1N 5HY
Telephone: +44 (0)20 7400 6500

Euro Mounts & Findings LLP
Birmingham branch
3 Hockley Street
Hockley, Birmingham
B18 6BL
Telephone: +44 (0)121 554 0111
Fax: +44 (0)121 554 0777
info@eurofinding.com
www.eurofindings.com

London branch
Antwerp House
26-27 Kirby Street
London
EC1N 8TE
Telephone: +44 (0)20 7404 5762
Fax: +44 (0)20 7831 6701
info@eurofindings.com
www.eurofindings.com

Rashbel UK
24-28 Hatton Wall
Hatton Garden, London
EC1N 8JH
Telephone: +44 (0)20 7831 5646
Fax: +44 (0)20 7831 5647
www.rashbel.com

UK STONE DEALERS

Marcia Lanyon Ltd
PO Box 370
London
W6 7NJ

Telephone: +44 (0)20 7602 2446
sales@marcialanyon.com
www.maricalanyon.co.uk

A.E Ward & Son Ltd
8 Albermarle Way
London
EC1V 4JB
Telephone: +44 (0)20 7253 4036
gemstones@aewgems.co.uk
www.aewgems.co.uk

R.M Weares & Co Ltd
PO Box 9
York
YO30 4QW
Telephone: +44 (0) 1904 693 933
gemstones@rmweare.com
www.rmweare.com

UK TOOL SUPPLIERS

Clerkenwell Screws Ltd
107-109 Clerkenwell Road
London
EC1R 5BY
Telephone: +44 (0)20 7405 1215

Clerkenwell Screws Ltd
Uxbridge branch
328 Uxbridge Road
London
W3 9QP
Telephone: +44 (0)20 8993 0454

Sutton Tools
Thomas Sutton (Birmingham) Ltd
83 Vittoria Street
Birmingham
B1 3NZ

Telephone: +44 (0)845 094 1884
info@suttontools.co.uk
www.suttontools.co.uk

Tilgear
Bridge House
69 Station Road
Cuffley, Herts
EN6 4TG
www.tilgear.info
Telephone: +44 (0)1707 873434

H.S. Walsh & Sons Limited
Beckenham branch (head office)
243 Beckenham Road
Beckenham, Kent
BR3 4TS
Telephone: +44 (0)20 8778 7061
www.hswalsh.com

Birmingham branch
1-2 Warstone Mews
Warstone Lane
Hockley, Birmingham
B18 6JB
Telephone: +44 (0)121 236 9346

London branch
44 Hatton Garden
London
EC1N 8ER
Telephone: +44 (0)20 7242 3711

UK CASTING COMPANIES

Euro-Cast (Birmingham) Ltd
48 Carver Street
Birmingham
B1 3AS
Telephone: +44 (0)121 233 2266

Fax: +44 (0)121 233 9731
info@euro-cast.co.uk
www.euro-cast.co.uk

Quality Castings
Unit 7
Canalside Studios
2-4 Orsman Road, London
N1 5QJ
Telephone: +44 (0)20 7729 3041
qcluk@aol.com
www.quality-castings.co.uk

UK POLISHERS & PLATERS

Elliot-Fitzpatrick Ltd
31 Hatton Garden
London
EC1 8DH
Telephone: +44 (0)20 7404 5124
Fax: +44 (0)20 7404 7528
elliot-fitzpatrick@aol.com
www.elliot-fitzpatrick.co.uk

UK WIRE COMPANIES

Wires.co.uk
18 Raven Road
South Woodford, London
E18 1HW
Telephone: +44 (0)20 8505 0002
Fax: +44 (0)20 8559 1114
dan@wires.co.uk
www.wires.co.uk

BASKET-MAKING EQUIPMENT AND FURTHER INFORMATION

www.basketassoc.org

UK ALUMINIUM SUPPLIERS

Aluminium Leicester
11 Putney Road West
Leicester
LE2 7TD
Telephone: +44 (0)116 255 3530

GSM Industrial Graphics (for buying in bulk)
Telephone: +44 (0)1993 776511
www.gsmindustrialgraphics.co.uk

Keraplate Ltd
Units 5-10
46 Holton Road
Holton Heath Trading Park
Poole, Dorset
BH16 6LT
Telephone: +44 (0)1202 622882
www.keraplate.co.uk

USA & GERMANY SUPPLIERS

Rio Grande (USA)
www.riogrande.com
Rio Grande is also a supplier of urethane rubber products and other die-forming tools.

Karl Fischer GmbH (Germany)
Berliner Strasse 18
Postfach 567
D-75105 Pforzheim
Tel: +49 (0) 72 31 31 0 31
info@fischer-pforzheim.de
www.fischer-pforzheim.de

Bibliography

BOOKS

Codina, Carles, *Handbook of Jewellery Techniques* (London: A&C Black
Publishers Ltd, Reprinted 2002, 2005)
    ISBN: 978-0-7136-5484-4

Kallenberg, Lawrence, *Modelling in Wax for Jewellery and Sculpture* (2nd edn)
(USA: Krause Publications, 2000, 1st edn pub 1981)
    ISBN: 0-87341-851-4

Kingsley, Susan, *Hydraulic Die Forming For Jewellers and Metalsmiths* (3rd edn)
(USA: Twenty-Ton Press, 2001)
    ISBN: 978-0-9635-8320-8

Mc Creight, Tim, *The Complete Metalsmith: An illustrated handbook* (Worcester,
Mass.: Davis Publications, Inc., 1991)
    ISBN: 0-87192-240-1

Untracht, Oppi, *Jewelry Concepts and Technology* (London: Robert Hale Ltd, 1st
pub 1982, reprinted 1987)
    ISBN: 0-7091-9616-4

USEFUL WEBSITES

www.acj.org.uk
www.cooksongold.com (Cookson's technical)
www.craftscouncil.org.uk
www.dictonary/reference.com
www.ganoksin.com
www.snagmetalsmith.org
www.thegoldsmiths.co.uk
www.wikipedia.org
www.professionaljeweler.com

newsletter@benchpeg.com (email to subscribe)

OTHER USEFUL BOOKS

Boothroyd, Angie, *Necklaces and Pendants* (London: A&C Black Publishers Ltd, 2007)
ISBN: 978-0-7136-7933-5

Gale, Emma and Little, Ann, *Teach Yourself Jewellery Making* (London: Hodder and Stoughton Ltd, 2000). For UK orders: orders@bookpoint.co.uk

Kulagowski, Yvonne, *The Earrings Book* (London: A&C Black Publishers Ltd, 2007)
ISBN: 978-0-7136-6505-5

Murphy, Kathie, *Design and Make Non-Precious Jewellery* (London: A&C Black Publishers Ltd, 2009)
ISBN 978-0-7136-8729-3.

Stöfer, Hans, *Wire Jewellery* (London: A&C Black Publishers Ltd, 2006)
ISBN: 978-0-7136-66342

Glossary of Terms

Anodising – The popular term given to the electrochemical process of forming an integral conversion coating on a metal surface, consisting of a stable oxide compound created for decorative or functional purposes (e.g. colouring aluminium) (source: Oppi Untracht, *Jewelry Concepts and Technology*).

Barrel polisher – A sealed barrel (or two) rotate on a motor. They are filled with a polishing compound and metal shots to burnish and polish any jewellery placed inside. To achieve a matt finish, you can exchange the metal shots and polishing compound and replace with a cutting compound and ceramic cones.

Beeswax – Used as a lubricant often for piercing saw blades. The blade is run through the beeswax once: too much will clog the teeth of the blade.

Binding wire – A soft thin wire, usually mild steel but also available in stainless steel. It is used to hold work together for soldering.

Blu-Tack® – The name used for a versatile, reusable, puttylike, pressure-sensitive adhesive.

Bobbin – A reel, cylinder or spool upon which thread or wire is wound.

Bodkin – A tapered steel tool with a wooden handle, similar to a thick blunt needle.

Borax – (Boric Acid) A mineral, a flux that helps remove oxide films and prevents further formation of oxides during heating. It comes in a cone form. You add water to a ceramic dish, rotate the cone around the dish and apply the paste to the metal join with a brush. Once heated it forms a glassy residue that should be removed by pickling.

Burnishing – A form of hand- or machine-polishing using a burnisher tool to apply friction and compression so as to make a metal surface shine without removing any metal.

Burr – This word has two meanings in jewellery terms. Firstly, a burr is the word for the irregular remaining edge or small lip that occurs when metal is removed. Secondly, a burr is also a word for a tool – for example, a ball burr, or a setting burr used in setting and/or wax-carving. These tools are mostly attached to a pendant motor.

Centrifugal casting – Casting that utilises centrifugal force within a spinning mould to force the metal against the walls. (source: wikipedia.com)

Crochet hook – A needle with a hook on the end, used in crocheting.

Chenier – Another word for tubing.

Chenier clamp – Steel clamping device for holding chenier while cutting. Clamping at 45° and 90° angles with a maximum capacity of 11 mm (0.43 in.) diameter.

Disc cutter – A metal tool that stamps out discs from metal of 1 mm (0.039 in.) maximum sheet thickness. Typically, this tool has eight size possibilities ranging from 5 to 16 mm (about 1.97 to 0.63 in.).

Drawplate – With the use of thick steel metal drawplates and drawtongs, wire can be drawn down into smaller sizes and various shapes. The drawplate has a range of holes and is available in different sizes. The drawplate can be clamped in a vice and the wire pulled through manually with drawtongs or used on a mechanical drawbench.

Emery paper – An abrasive paper used to clean, texture and polish surfaces.

Fabricated – To make by assembling parts or sections.

Fire stain – An oxide of copper that forms on sterling-silver and gold alloys when it has been heated. It appears as a dark grey patch, or patches, just below the surface of the metal, and can be removed by filing.

Flux – A liquid applied to a metal join to allow the solder to flow and help prevent oxidisation.

Fly press – A manually operated metalworking machine tool which works by using a coarse screw to convert the gross rotation of an overhead handle into a small downward movement with the force considerably multiplied. The overhead handle is usually counterbalanced with a flyweight, which helps to maintain the momentum and thrust of the tool as it punches or compresses the material. (source: wikipedia.com)

Fusing – The joining of metals by means of heat without using solder.

Gauge – The thickness or diameter of various (usually thin) objects. This word is usually applied to the thickness of sheet metal or the diameter of a wire or screw.

Ground maize cob – A drying medium that absorbs moisture, it can be purchased in 1 kg (2 lb 3 oz) bags from suppliers such as Cookson, and is relatively inexpensive.

Honeycomb board – Used to solder on, this is a ceramic block with small holes through it to help dissipate the heat from the work piece. It is acid-resistant and can be heated up to 1093°C.

Jump ring – A small plain ring, usually not joined, used for connecting links.

Mallet – A hammer-shaped tool, made of a material that will not mark metal too much. Mallets can be made of rawhide, wood, plastic, paper or horn.

Malleable – Capable of being shaped or formed, such as by hammering or pressure. (source: wikipedia.com)

Mandrel – Made of cast iron or sometimes wood, this is a large tapered form, usually either round or oval, ideal for shaping bangles. Ring mandrels (used for rings, of course) are much smaller.

Micro-motor – Like a pendant motor, its electronically balanced for minimal vibration and maximum operating comfort. Ideal for intricate precision work.

Mokume-gane – First made in 17th-century Japan, this is 'a mixed-metal laminate with distinctive layered patterns. Literally translating as 'wood-eye metal', the name was borrowed from one type of pattern created in the forging of swords and other edged weapons'. (source: wikipedia.com)

Oxide – A dark stain on metal, usually silver, that occurs after prolonged exposure to air.

Oxidise – To blacken metal, usually silver, with chemicals.

Pin vice – A tool used to hold small pieces of wire, drill bits or burrs.

Pi (π) – Used as the symbol for the ratio of the circumference of a circle to its diameter. The ratio itself: 3.141592+ (approximately 3.14)

Pallions – Tiny pieces of solder, approximately 1 mm (0.039in.) square that are cut, usually with tin snips, from a strip of solder.

Planishing – Flattens or smoothes out metal surfaces using a special hammer and technique.

Reticulation – This occurs when metal is heated almost to melting point, as the surface begins to turn molten and crinkles. Heat is then removed and the surface solidifies, leaving a decorative, rippled final surface.

RT blanking tool – This process was invented by Roger Taylor, a practising designer-jeweller, and is subject to British Patent No. 1594396. The tool is usually made from a hard metal, such as steel, and is simply made by piercing the metal at an angle, thus creating a tight opening in which to slot thin metal so as to stamp out the pierced shape. The blanking tools are suitable for use by hand with a hammer. It is also possible to buy a machine called the RT Blanking System from H.S. Walsh (see the list of suppliers) that will assist in making this tool for you.

Safety pickle – A weak acid solution used to remove flux and oxides from the metal, safety pickle can be purchased from suppliers. Alum can also be used as a pickle.

Scotch-Brite pad™ – Made by 3M products, this is a kitchen scourer that when rubbed against metal creates a matt, brushed finish.

Solder – A non-ferrous alloy available in many metal types - for example, silver, gold and platinum - crucially, it has a lower melting point than the metal to be joined.

Soldering – The term used for the joining together of two pieces of metal using a special metal alloy, called solder. When the metal is heated to a certain temperature the solder melts across the join, then solidifies again as it cools.

Specific gravity – 'The ratio of the weight of any volume of a substance whose standard is water for solids and liquids, and air or hydrogen for gases, taken at the same temperature'. (source: Oppi Untracht, *Jewelry Concepts and Technology*, see Bibliography)

Swarf – Fine metallic filings or shavings removed by a cutting tool.

True – To make exact.

Urethane – A tough rubber-like substance, but said to be more flexible and forgiving than rubber. Urethane returns to its original shape after use, and can be reused thousands of times. The rubber used in John Moore's project is red, which is the hardest at approximately 95 durometers (a way of measuring hardness).

Vernier gauge – An instrument to enable accurate measuring.

Vice – A device used for securely holding work.

Work-hardened – The process by which metal becomes harder and more brittle as it is repeatedly hammered, rolled, drawn, twisted or bent.

Index